T0110743

ACKNOWLEDGMENTS

To the hundreds of experts — parents, authors, organizations, doctors and psychologists — who helped me with my research. Thank you for giving me your time and answering my innumerable questions.

To my agent, Jane Dystel, for her advice, encouragement and perseverance.

To my editor, Dona Chernoff, for picking this project up in the middle and seeing it to a fine conclusion. And to Joann Foster and Donna Ruvituso, for helping smooth the way.

To Karen Todaro and Barbara Gillespie, for helping get this project off the ground from a great idea to a real book.

To Maggie Meehan and Dan Starer, for their help and friendship from the start (and great editing tips, too).

To Dr. Max Van Gilder, for reading the book in its early stages and offering many helpful suggestions (and lots of dry humor in the margins). And thanks to Elaine, Ivette, Sandy and everyone in Dr. Van Gilder's office for always giving my children the best of care.

To Debbe Heller, for her immeasurable time, effort and dedication to making this book and my dream come true.

To Dolly and Harold Fishman, for bringing up a son to be a great husband and father. And to Andrew, Jackie and Theo, for being my prime audience.

And finally, to all of my friends for listening to me talk endlessly about my book long before it was one — here it is at last!

THANK YOU ALL.

DEDICATION

To my "expert" parents, Thelma and Mike Kandel, for always believing I could do it.

To Gary, for his unfailing love, support and friendship.

To Ryan and Jared, for teaching me each day how extraordinary it is to be a parent.

CONTENTS

INTRODUCTION

When my first son, Ryan, was born 8 years ago I found that I had dozens of questions every day about what to do and when to do it — questions I often didn't think important enough to call my pediatrician about.

So what did I do? I called my mom; I ran next door to ask my neighbor, a much more experienced mother than I; or I searched through the many child care books that filled my shelves.

But the books frustrated me. I had to scan numerous references in indexes and read pages and pages of text to find any answers.

That's why *The Expert Parent* was born.
My mother, Thelma, and I realized that while parents everywhere crave information, tips and advice to help them parent, most of them don't have time to wade through copious index listings and search through dozens of pages in a book when their baby is crying and they need a quick answer NOW!

The goal of *The Expert Parent* is to provide a handy reference guide that clearly and concisely compiles the most important information busy parents need to know, from all the experts in the know.

The book will give you the basics in minutes — fast facts, efficiently organized to make it a snap to get answers to your questions on every facet of raising, feeding, educating and playing with children from birth through age 5. Plus, we will tell you where we got the information so you know where to go to get more.

To write *The Expert Parent* we went directly to the experts. We interviewed hundreds of authors, doctors, psychologists, and people at organizations and associations specializing in the basic information parents need every day to do their most important job. Some of those include:

✶ Renowned sleep expert **Dr. Richard Ferber**, author of *Solve Your Child's Sleep Problems*, for sleep solutions.

✶ **La Leche League** for nursing advice.

✶ **The American Association of Poison Control Centers** for advice on hazardous products to beware.

✶ **Heidi Murkoff**, one of the best-selling authors of *What to Expect When You're Expecting,* for tips on what to pack in your diaper bag.

We also provide advice on subjects you don't usually find in most parenting books:

✶ How to choose a bicycle helmet, from the **Bicycle Helmet Safety Institute.**

✶ How to make your own bubbles and play dough, from **The Tightwad Gazette** newsletter.

✶ When to worry about stuttering, from the **Stuttering Foundation of America.**

✶ How to tell a bedtime story, from the **National Storytelling Association.**

Our sidebars and resource section list hundreds of phone numbers and addresses so you can get catalogs, newsletters, reading lists and other information from the people we interviewed.

After doing our research, we've become parenting "experts" of sorts — though we're still learning every day. Here's a list of the top dozen things my mother and I think every parent needs to become an "expert parent":

* Love

* Patience

* Optimism

* An open mind

* Dreams to share and stories to tell

* A sense of fun and retaining a little bit of "child" in yourself

* The power to foster self-esteem

* The sense to ask for help

* Common sense and good instincts

* The self-control to step back and let children do for themselves and learn from their own mistakes

* A sense of authority so their children know their limits, but the ability to let them win some of the battles

* Lots of luck

The birth of your baby is the start of the most challenging, difficult, wonderful and exciting adventure of your life. Remember: there is more than one right way to do just about everything when it comes to parenting. What works for one parent and one child doesn't always work for another, and what works one day doesn't always work the next.

Parenting is a daily educational experience. As a result, there's no such thing as a "perfect" parent. "Expert" parents simply know where to go to get the answers to their questions. Since babies don't come with instructions, let *The Expert Parent* guide you on your way to raising children who are healthy and confident, curious and challenged, safe and happy.

Enjoy! — Bethany Kandel

How to use *The Expert Parent*

Here are some tips on how we've organized our material:

 **The expert:** The hand pointing at the bottom of the page shows you the name of the expert person or organization we interviewed for the information that precedes it. If you want to know how to contact this expert, turn to the resource section at the end of the book where you'll find their phone number and address.

 Whom to call: The telephone receiver denotes important related phone numbers on the subject.

Footnote: These provide a fun fact or added bit of information on the corresponding subject.

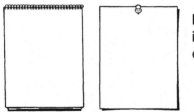 **Pushpin or spiral notebook:** Within these icons is more in-depth information on the topic or on a related subject.

Note: The pronouns "he" and "she" are used in alternate chapters in order not to show preference for either gender. "She" is used in chapter one; "he" in chapter two; etc.

Chapter One

GETTING STARTED

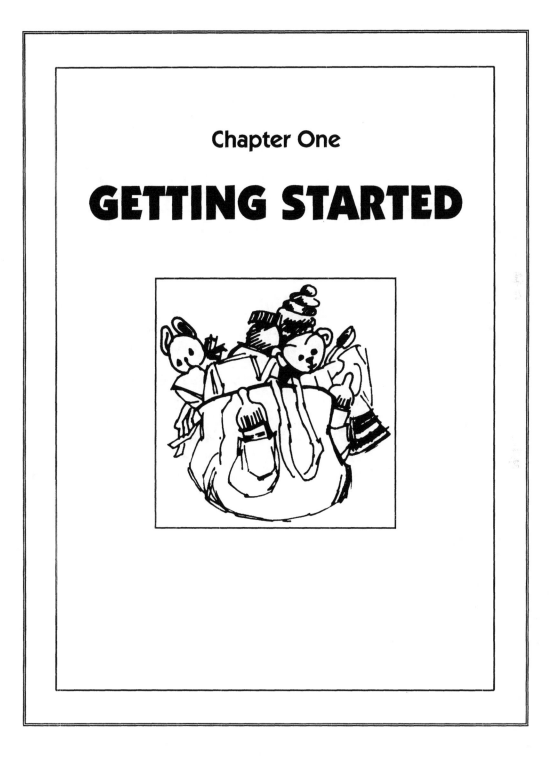

One of your most important decisions as a parent is the choice of a pediatrician; someone who will provide good care for your child, listen to your concerns, and answer even your dumbest questions.

How to choose a pediatrician

Dr. Bob Arnot, chief medical correspondent for the CBS Evening News, suggests working backward: Find the best medical center for pediatrics in your area; get the names of affiliated pediatricians, and then ask your own doctors, friends and relatives for recommendations.

Once you've found some candidates who meet your initial criteria, interview several to "get a sense of chemistry" before making a decision. Start looking near the end of your pregnancy so your doctor can be the one to release your baby from the hospital.

You want a pediatrician who . . .

★ Can not only help you guard against disease and catch problems early but is plugged in to a myriad of resources and experts in case you ever need them.

★ Lets you be part of decisions and doesn't brush you off with a "let me worry about that" attitude.

★ Is supportive of your parenting role and is open to different opinions or approaches.

Questions to ask

★ What are your office hours? (Weekend and evening hours may be important.)

★ What are your fees?

★ Do you accept my insurance?

★ Ask a solo practitioner: Who covers for you? Ask a group practice: Does each doctor see her own patients?

★ How are emergencies handled?

★ How are phone calls returned?

★ Do you assess a baby's emotional development and behavior as well as physical growth?

★ What is your philosophy or style of practice?

★ What is your view on breast-feeding versus bottle-feeding? Demand versus scheduled feeding? (And other baby care issues.)

What to look for . . .

★ Do you feel comfortable asking the doctor questions? Does the doctor take time to address your concerns?

★ Is the office staff friendly and helpful? Is the waiting room child-friendly? Crowded?

★ Is the office convenient for quick sick visits?

★ Talk to other parents in the waiting room for the real low-down: How long do they usually wait for scheduled or sick visits? Does the doctor return calls quickly? Were they satisfied with any emergency care? How do their children respond to the doctor?

 THE EXPERT: Bob Arnot, M.D., author of *The Best Medicine: How to Choose the Top Doctors, the Top Hospitals, and the Top Treatments* (Addison-Wesley, 1993).

The arrival of a sibling is likely to trigger ambivalent emotions and behaviors in your firstborn. Smooth the adjustment by preparing your older child during your pregnancy with information and emotional support. Reassure your child that Mommy and Daddy have enough love for more than one child.

Preparing your child for a sibling

During pregnancy

★ Don't break the news to your child until your pregnancy becomes physically obvious.

★ Tie the due date to an event your child can relate to: "after your birthday" or "once camp begins."

★ Reinforce your firstborn's important family role. Say "You're going to become a big sister/brother," instead of announcing, "Mommy is having a baby."

★ Involve your child in the pregnancy and preparations: let her listen to the heartbeat, feel the baby's kicks, and help set up the baby's room.

★ Read books about birth, babies and siblings.

★ Tell stories about the excitement of your firstborn's birth.

★ Look through her baby photos together.

★ Explain that newborns mostly sleep, eat and cry, so she won't expect an instant playmate.

★ Move your older child to a new room or a big bed several months before the baby's birth.

★ Have your older child choose which of her old toys, clothes or blankets her sibling might like. Respect her desire not to share some special things.

4

Before you go to the hospital

★ Explain that Mommy has to go to the hospital to deliver the baby and you'll be home in a few days. Tell your child who will take care of her while you're gone.

★ Ask her to draw pictures to decorate your hospital room.

Once baby is born

★ Give your firstborn a special gift from the baby — a T-shirt or button announcing, "I'm a big sister/brother," a toy or a book.

★ Refer to the newborn as "our baby."

★ Maintain rituals like bedtime stories and Sunday brunch with Dad to help your child adjust to other changes.

★ Help your child express any negative feelings about the baby with words, playacting with dolls or drawing pictures.

★ Spend time alone with your older child.

★ Include your firstborn: read her a story while nursing baby; let her hand you a diaper at changing time, etc.

★ Give small gifts to your older child when baby presents arrive.

★ Encourage visitors to pay attention to both children. Say: "Let me tell you what my big girl/boy did today. . . ."

★ Expect some regression. It will soon pass.

THE EXPERT: Christine Heusner, R.N., sibling preparation teacher, Parent/Family Education, St. Luke's-Roosevelt Hospital, New York.

Animals, too, need to adjust to a new family member, especially when they've been the "only child."

Preparing the family pet

Before baby is born

★ Get any necessary shots and flea, tick or worm treatments. Make sure pet is spayed or neutered.

★ Expose your cat or dog to babies and toddlers to prepare her for the new smells and sounds.

★ Hold a baby or a doll while your pet is nearby and talk to her in reassuring tones. Use praise and positive reinforcement for appropriate behavior.

★ Let your pet inspect the nursery.

Once baby is born

★ Send baby's T-shirt home from the hospital so your pet can get used to the newcomer's scent.

★ When you return home, have someone else hold the infant while you greet your pet. Slowly introduce the baby, praising and reassuring your pet. Don't be surprised if a cat goes into hiding.

★ Never leave an animal alone with an infant, but don't isolate your pet from baby. Reduce competitive feelings by letting your pet stay near while you change or nurse the baby and give attention to both.

★ Spend some time each day alone with your pet.

★ Don't let pets climb into the crib or onto your lap while you are holding baby.

★ Animals are creatures of habit; maintain normal mealtimes and walks.

For dogs only

✶ Train your dog to sit, stay, and lie down on command.

✶ Call a professional trainer if your dog growls when you approach her food or guards objects (a potential danger to a crawling baby), has a predatory drive (she can view the baby as prey), or has a tendency to bite or snap.

For cats only

✶ Train your cat not to jump into your lap. Place her beside you; pet her and offer a treat. Pay attention to the cat only when she is next to you, not on you.

✶ Train your cat to avoid certain areas by putting double-stick tape on the changing table, crib and carriage.

✶ Use tight-fitting mosquito netting to prevent your cat from jumping into the crib or bassinet while baby sleeps.

✶ Keep the litter box clean and off-limits to a soon-to-be crawling baby. Wash your hands after handling.

 THE EXPERT: The American Society for the Prevention of Cruelty to Animals.

The quantity and variety of baby paraphernalia available are overwhelming and expensive.

What to buy for baby

Before buying any major equipment, ask friends and relatives which brands and models worked for them and what extras they loved or, on the other hand, could have lived without.   Ask if they have anything you can borrow and check tag sales for secondhand items. Make sure anything new or used is certified with a seal from the Juvenile Products Manufacturers Association (JPMA) for assurance that it meets safety standards.

Buying or borrowing secondhand

✴ Ask the age of the item. Make sure it meets current safety standards.

✴ Check for missing hardware, loose threads, strings, holes or tears.

✴ Get original instructions or call the manufacturer for a copy.

Before using any equipment

✴ Read all instructions.

✴ Mail in warranty or buyer registration cards so you'll be notified in case of a recall.

✴ Always fasten safety straps and tightly secure locking mechanisms.

To determine whether an item has been recalled by the U.S. Consumer Product Safety Commission, call the manufacturer or the CPSC hotline: 800-638-CPSC.

THE EXPERT: Juvenile Products Manufacturers Association.

Buying a car seat

You can wait to buy almost everything else for baby, except the car seat. Buy or borrow one before the baby is born for a safe ride home from the hospital.

✶ Choose either an infant-only seat or a convertible infant/toddler seat. The former is designed to face rearward in a semi-reclining position for babies from birth to 1 year and up to 20 pounds. The disadvantage is that you have to buy another seat when baby outgrows it. The advantage is that it's more comfortable for an infant, especially a very small one. Some models can be removed from their bases to double as infant carriers or can be locked onto shopping carts.

✶ The convertible seat, for babies from birth to 40 pounds, can be used in the reclining, rearward position at birth, and later turned around in an upright, forward-facing position when your child turns 1 year or weighs 20 pounds.

When considering a used car seat be sure it:

- Is less than 10 years old.
- Has never been involved in a crash.
- Has all its parts and instructions.
- Has not been recalled.

If you have questions about how to properly use your car seat, call the manufacturer or SafetyBeltSafe U.S.A.: 800-745-SAFE. To check whether a car seat has ever been recalled, call the National Highway Traffic Safety Administration Auto Safety Hotline: 800-424-9393 with the manufacturer, year and model number.

THE EXPERT: SafetyBeltSafe U.S.A.

Safety Tips

Crib

• Never place a crib near drape or blind cords.
• Don't hang any stringed object, like toys or laundry bag, on crib where baby could get entangled.
• Remove crib gyms and mobiles when baby can push up on hands and knees. Remove bumper pads when baby can pull up to a standing position.
• Do not use pillows; infants can suffocate and older babies can climb on them and fall out.
• If buying secondhand, make sure no slats are broken or missing. Remove or cut off any decorative knobs or tall corner posts.

Buying a crib

★ Purchase a crib built after 1974 when government safety standards were enacted.

★ Slats must be spaced less than 2 3/8 inches apart.

★ There should be no cutouts in the headboard or footboard that could trap an infant's head.

★ Corner posts should extend no more than 1/16 of an inch above the end panel to prevent entanglement of clothing or cords around the neck.

★ Crib mattress should fit snugly so that two adult fingers cannot fit between mattress and crib side.

★ Drop-side latches should securely hold sides in raised position and not be easily released by a child.

★ All screws, bolts and hardware must be smooth, free of sharp edges, and tightly in place.

THE EXPERT: The Danny Foundation.

Buying a carriage/stroller

Consider your lifestyle when buying a carriage or stroller. If you'll be in and out of a vehicle, choose a lightweight, easily collapsible model; if you plan long walks, you may want a sturdier model with large, shock-absorbing wheels for a smooth ride. Take several models for a test spin around the store, assessing brakes, maneuverability and folding ease. Look for:

✳ A carriage that converts to an upright stroller.

✳ Easy one-hand folding. Practice opening and closing before you take the baby out for a spin.

✳ Swiveling wheels and brakes that lock securely. Ask if the manufacturer makes replacement wheels.

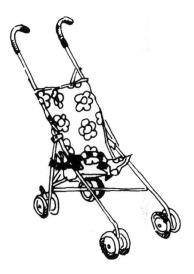

✳ Ample storage space. (Hanging items on the handles can cause it to tip.)

✳ Comfortable handle height, or ask if extenders are available.

✳ Safety straps that are easy for you to latch but difficult for baby to open.

✳ Handy extras: canopy, umbrella or all-weather cover to shield baby from the elements; removable, washable seat cover.

 THE EXPERT: U.S. Consumer Product Safety Commission and the Juvenile Products Manufacturers Association.

Buying a walker

Walkers are currently very controversial and there is even an effort to ban them. The U.S. Consumer Product Safety Commission estimates that more children are injured in walkers than by any other nursery product. Safer alternatives are the new, nonambulatory versions that rock but don't roll. If you do decide to use a walker, never use near stairs and follow all safety tips. Look for:

★ A wide wheel base for stability.

★ Coil springs and hinges with protective coverings.

Buying a toy box

★ Choose a toy box without a top or choose one with a lightweight, removable lid.

★ If you use one with a hinged lid, be sure it has a spring support that holds the lid open at any angle.

★ To protect a child who may climb inside a toy box with a hinged lid, it should have ventilation holes and a lid that doesn't latch.

Safety Tips

Walker

• Always keep a baby in a walker in your sight.

• Use walkers only on smooth surfaces. Edges of carpets, rugs or raised thresholds can cause them to tip.

• Make sure there are gates at the top of all stairways or keep stairway doors closed.

• Childproof all shelves and tabletops that can be reached from the walker. Keep wires and drape cords out of reach.

THE EXPERT: U.S. Consumer Product Safety Commission and the Juvenile Products Manufacturers Association.

Buying a high chair

★ Make sure there are both waist and crotch straps.

★ Look for a wide, stable base.

★ A folding high chair must have effective locking devices to keep from collapsing.

Buying a gate

★ Avoid old-fashioned, accordion-style folding gates — the diamond-shaped openings within, and large V-shaped openings along the top, can entrap baby's head or limbs.

★ Buy a gate with a pressure bar or other fastener that can resist the weight of a child.

Buying a playpen

★ Mesh should have a small weave, with less than 1/4-inch openings, and be securely attached to top rail and floorplate.

★ Wooden slats should be spaced no more than 2 3/8 inches apart.

Safety Tips

High chair
•If you suspect a secondhand wooden high chair may contain lead paint, strip it and repaint with a lead-free one.
• Keep high chairs away from table, walls or counters that baby can use to push off from and topple chair.

Playpen
• Never leave baby in a mesh playpen with the drop-side down.
• Never tie anything across the top or to the sides with a string longer than six inches.

THE EXPERT: U.S. Consumer Product Safety Commission and the Juvenile Products Manufacturers Association.

*If you are
going back to
work or need
child care by a
certain date,
give yourself at
least a month
to find the
right caregiver
or center
for your child.*

How to choose a caregiver

Some of the child care options to consider include having a caregiver come to your home, taking your child to a day care center, or going to family child care in someone else's home. Every caregiver and center is different, so check out several for comparison before making a decision.

Even if you're only looking for an occasional sitter, many of the following guidelines and questions will come in handy.

★ Create a job description: required days and hours, wages, duties, etc. Decide which are absolutes and where there's flexibility.

★ Screen applicants/centers by phone to find those that meet your basic requirements. Keep notes of the information you receive and your initial reactions.

★ Go with your gut. You must feel comfortable and confident with your choice.

When hiring a caregiver, be aware of the government's "Nanny Tax," which requires payment of Social Security taxes for domestic employees. Check with an accountant or call your state department of taxation for information and current requirements.

Questions to ask

What type of job are you looking for?

What experience do you have?

What is your education in early child development?

Do you have CPR or first aid training?

Why did you leave your previous job?

What were your responsibilities? Did you have any trouble meeting them?

How did you handle a tough situation?

What was your relationship like with your previous employer?

How flexible are you when a change of scheduling occurs?

What would you do if we disagreed about something?

Do you smoke or drink?

Do you have a driver's license?

Do you have any health problems? How many days did you miss last year?

Do you believe in letting a baby cry, or would you pick her up immediately?

How would you discipline a child? Do you believe in spanking?

How would you keep an infant/toddler occupied?

What television shows do you think are appropriate for children? What are your favorite children's books?

What would you do while my child is sleeping?

What would you do if you found my child holding an open pill bottle? If my child was choking? If she appeared sick during the day?

How long a commitment can you make?

 THE EXPERT: National Association of Child Care Resource and Referral Agencies.

Checking references

Before hiring a caregiver, get references from at least three former employers. Ask them to be candid. Listen to how they respond to your questions, as well as to what they say. Ask:

Caregiver Contract

Once you hire a caregiver, write a contract that you both sign. Include hours, salary, vacations, paid holidays, sick days, overtime, and when raises will be discussed. Clarify any household duties. Request two weeks' notice if the caregiver decides to leave. Such an agreement may not be legally binding, but it may help if a dispute or question arises.

★ What sort of relationship did the caregiver have with you and your children?

★ What did/didn't you like about her?

★ Why did the caregiver leave? If she left you, did she give you time to find a replacement?

★ Did she follow directions?

★ Was she responsible? Punctual? Tidy?

★ Was it a problem if you came home late from work?

★ How were disagreements handled?

★ How did the caregiver handle an emergency?

★ Is there anything I should know about her?

★ Would you hire her again?

For assistance in finding a child care resource and referral agency in your area, call the Child Care Aware National Information Line: 800-424-2246.

THE EXPERT: National Association of Child Care Resource and Referral Agencies.

Prepare your caregiver for an emergency

✱ Always leave a number where you can be reached and one for a friend, relative or neighbor.

✱ Post phone numbers for police, fire, Poison Control, ambulance, pediatrician and dentist by all telephones.

✱ Also post your address and clear directions on how to locate your house, plus the name of the nearest hospital that offers the best emergency care for children. (Not all emergency rooms are equipped to treat children properly.)

✱ Show where to find syrup of ipecac and leave instructions to always call the Poison Control Center before administering.

✱ Prepare and sign a consent form authorizing emergency treatment for your children. Unless the situation is life-threatening, doctors will not treat a child without parental permission. The form should state that any licensed physician, dentist or hospital may provide necessary emergency medical service to the child at the request of the person bearing the consent form.

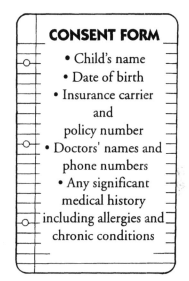

CONSENT FORM

- Child's name
- Date of birth
- Insurance carrier and policy number
- Doctors' names and phone numbers
- Any significant medical history including allergies and chronic conditions

To receive a sample consent form, send a stamped, self-addressed envelope to Consent Form American College of Emergency Physicians 1111 19th Street NW Suite 650 Washington, DC 20036.

☞ THE EXPERT: American College of Emergency Physicians.

What your caregiver needs to know

If you're returning to work outside the home, have a new caregiver come in several days beforehand. You can show her around the house, demonstrate your routines, and let her and baby get used to each other while you're around.

When hiring a new sitter for an occasional evening out, also have her arrive at least a half hour before you leave and provide the same information.

✳ Show all entrances and exits, fire/burglar alarms, first aid supplies, fuse box, flashlights, emergency phone numbers, any off-limits areas, plus where you keep diapers, clothing, bottles, formula, food and snacks.

✳ Review feeding, napping and bedtime routines.

✳ Note whether baby uses a special pacifier, blanket or comfort toy.

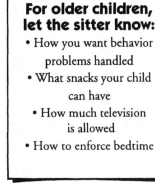

For older children, let the sitter know:

- How you want behavior problems handled
- What snacks your child can have
- How much television is allowed
- How to enforce bedtime

✸ Explain how you want baby picked up, diapered, fed and burped. Do you want baby picked up anytime she cries?

✸ Advise what to do if baby won't fall asleep.

✸ Write down how much, how often, and how to give any medications.

✸ Set rules on visitors and use of phone and television. Explain that smoking and alcohol are never allowed.

✸ Discuss what to do in case of emergency or fire.

✸ Leave a number where you can be reached and give a time when you will return home.

To enroll your sitter (aged 11 to 13) in a Safe Sitter safety and child care skills training program in your area, call 800-255-4089, or inquire whether your local hospital or American Red Cross chapter offers a similar class.

 THE EXPERT: Patricia Keener, M.D., founder and medical director, Safe Sitter, Inc.

Choosing day care

Before putting your child in a day care center, make sure the provider is licensed. Check references. Visit when parents drop off or pick up their children and talk to them. Decide if you think the size of the group will allow your child to get the individual attention she needs.

Questions to ask

Who operates the center?

What are the credentials of staff members? How long have they worked there?

What is the child-staff ratio?

Will my child have a specific caregiver?

What are your hours?

What age children do you care for?

What is the separation policy?

What meals/snacks are provided?

Do all children have up-to-date immunizations?

What is your discipline policy?

Do parents get updates/conferences on their child?

How will my child spend each day?

How do you deal with sick children? Emergencies?

What to look for . . .

Observe the day care center when you have a scheduled appointment and also visit when the staff is not expecting you.

✱ Staff and children should wash their hands before and after they eat and after they go to the bathroom. Staff should wash up before preparing children's food and after changing diapers or wiping a child's nose.

✱ There should be a designated diaper-changing area. Changing tables should be wiped after each use or fresh paper liners used.

✱ The center should smell fresh and be clean. Toys should be sanitized regularly.

✱ Cold food should be refrigerated until served and warm meals should be eaten immediately after heating.

✱ Do the children seem happy and busy?

✱ How do the adults respond to children's questions and problems?

✱ Is the room child-friendly? Is there enough room for energetic children to move around? Are bathroom facilities child-sized? Is the room childproofed? Are first aid supplies on hand?

 THE EXPERT: National Association of Child Care Resource and Referral Agencies.

Choosing family child care

When choosing family child care in a home setting, focus on many of the same things that you would at a day care center.

Questions to ask

Are you licensed?

Are you affiliated with any agency or group of family child care providers?

Are you trained in child development? CPR? First aid?

How long have you cared for children in your home?

How many children do you care for? What are their ages? (State guidelines vary from five to nine children per adult.)

Do you have your own children? What are their ages? Are they home during the day?

What happens if you or your children get sick?

Do you work alone? If you have assistants, what are their credentials?

How much space in your home is used for family child care?

How does your family feel about your business?

What to look for . . .

★ Examine the physical space and safety of the home, yard and equipment.

★ Is the home childproofed and clean? Are there safety gates on stairs? Smoke detectors? Fire extinguishers? Window guards? Do children have their own cups and towels, or are disposables available?

★ Does the caregiver promote self-esteem by displaying the children's artwork?

★ Watch how the caregiver interacts and relates to children of all ages. Is she warm and nurturing with infants? Does she offer a stimulating environment and appropriate activities for older children?

 THE EXPERT: National Association for Family Child Care.

Postpartum depression

Although having a baby is a joyous time, 50 to 75 percent of new moms have some feelings of melancholy in the first weeks after birth. Not surprising: your hormones are in flux, your body is recovering, you're surviving on less sleep, and you're adjusting to your new role. These "baby blues" usually disappear, yet about 10 percent of new moms suffer a postpartum depression that can last for months. Symptoms may range from mild to severe. Contact a local support group and talk to your doctor to get treatment or counseling if you continue to have any or all of the following symptoms:

✶ Severe mood swings and crying for no apparent reason

✶ Loss of interest in things that used to bring pleasure

✶ Marked change in appetite

✶ Insomnia

✶ Panic attacks

✶ Extreme anxiety about the baby or lack of concern

✶ Feelings of inadequacy, sadness, guilt or helplessness that disrupt your ability to function

✶ Thoughts of harming yourself or your baby

For information on postpartum depression and a list of local therapists and support groups call Depression After Delivery: 800-944-4773, or Postpartum Support International: 805-967-7636.

THE EXPERT: Depression After Delivery.

How to start a mothers' group

How to organize

✶ Post signs in your pediatrician's office, supermarket, playground and local baby store asking new mothers to call if they want to join a group.

✶ Print cards with your name and phone number to give to new moms you spot around your neighborhood.

✶ Contact the women in your prenatal exercise or birthing class.

Once you organize

✶ Pick a regular time and take turns meeting at each other's homes or at a local playground.

✶ Establish guidelines, including a policy on sick children, sharing diaper supplies, snacks, etc.

✶ Meet informally or choose topics for discussion. Find an occasional guest speaker: a local La Leche League representative, a childproofing expert or a baby massage therapist.

✶ Rent and watch a child care video together.

✶ If your group grows, look for space to set up a mothers' center at your local Y, church or synagogue.

Forming a mothers' group can help new moms avoid isolation, find friends, and share baby care information. As your babies grow they will enjoy the camaraderie as well.

Working moms can meet evenings or weekends or start a lunchtime group at work.

THE EXPERT: National Association of Mothers' Centers.

Babies change and grow so quickly, it's nice to preserve memories along the way. Here are simple ways to create a family archive by keeping a record of baby's daily life, as well as major milestones, beyond the baby book and home videos.

Making memories

★ Create a time capsule to mark baby's birth. Fill a box with the birth announcement, photos, hospital bracelet, newly minted coins, newly issued stamps, a fashion catalog, news magazine, and political campaign button. Open it on your child's 18th birthday.

★ Keep a calendar or blank journal near your rocking chair or nightstand to make notes about life with baby and your feelings as a new parent.

★ Hold a photo session on baby's monthly birthday every month for the first year. Take a picture in the same spot with the same props (next to a favorite stuffed animal) or with one (unlit) candle in a marshmallow for each month baby is celebrating. Frame the series for a visual record of baby's rapid growth.

★ Post a piece of paper on the refrigerator to keep a running list of each new word your learning talker says and the date she said it.

✸ Write an annual letter to baby, noting "firsts," new friends and favorite foods. Mention world events and include a list of what's "hot" that year, from movies to fashions, even the price of a hot dog or comic book.

✸ Trace hands and feet on each birthday.

✸ Save the newspaper from the day baby is born and on each subsequent birthday.

✸ Tape-record your growing child; include baby's early gurgles and coos, first words, sentences and songs.

✸ Photograph baby's smile as each new tooth appears. Later, pair them in an album with smile pictures as baby teeth fall out.

✸ Sew pieces of baby's blanket, favorite T-shirts and outfits into a keepsake quilt or wall hanging.

Let the President of the United States welcome your baby with a congratulatory note. Send baby's birth date and the names of parents and child to
The White House
Greetings Office
Room 39
1600 Pennsylvania Ave. NW
Washington, DC 20500.

THE EXPERT: Judy Lawrence, educator and counselor; author of *Our Family Memories: Highlights of Our Times Together* (Blue Sky Marketing, Inc., 1995).

How to stay in touch with the grandparents

Once upon a time, grandparents lived upstairs or across the street. These days, it's just as likely that they live thousands of miles away. But out of sight doesn't have to mean out of mind. Here are ways to keep in touch.

For parents and children

★ Buy the grandparents an expandable photo album and keep a pack of empty pages for yourself. Get double prints when you develop a roll of film; then put a set right into the album pages and mail.

★ Assemble an album of photos of Grandma and Grandpa, their house and their pets. Look at it often so your child stays familiar with them between visits.

★ Mail occasional tape recordings of baby's early gurgles and as she grows have her sing songs and tell stories.

★ Send a continuous stream of your child's artwork. Grandparents like to cover their refrigerators, too.

★ Include grandparents in everyday life: send photos of your child and her friends, copies of report cards, and sports and school schedules.

★ To get your child to talk to her grandparents on the phone, help her learn a joke, rhyme or riddle to recite. Give her a photo of them to look at while she's talking.

Suggest these to the grandparents

✴ Plant a tree when your grandchild is born: take photos of its growth and let her tend it when she visits.

✴ Tape-record yourself singing lullabies or telling bedtime stories so you can be with your grandchild every night.

✴ Children love mail: send postcards, letters, cartoons and packages with child-sized hotel toiletries, stickers and other treats.

✴ Send jokes: your grandchild has to call for the punchline.

✴ Start a continuous story: write a few paragraphs and mail it to your grandchild to continue. Mom can always read it to her and take dictation for the response.

✴ Send contributions to a dress-up box: your old scarves, ties, hats, gloves, petticoats and jewelry.

Help your baby's grandparents feel connected to their new roles; join them in the Caring Grandparents of America: 800-441-7181 or Young Grandparents' Club: 913-642-8296.

THE EXPERT: Sunie Levin, founder of the Young Grandparents' Club and author of *You and Your Grandchildren* (Price Stern Sloan, 1991).

Chapter Two

NEWBORN
BIRTH–SIX MONTHS

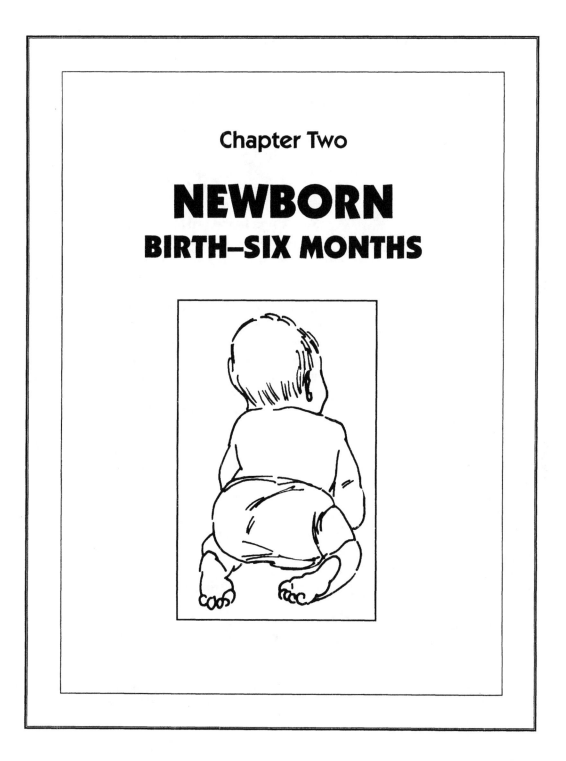

DAILY CARE

Bathing baby

Sponge baths are all baby needs until the umbilical cord falls off (up to two weeks after birth), and until a boy's circumcision has healed (about one week).

After that — until baby crawls or eats solids — he needs to be bathed only two or three times a week, and shampooed once or twice a week. Between baths, use a washcloth to keep baby's face, ears, neck folds and genitals clean. Soap is not necessary for infants. When you use it, choose sensitive-skin types with mild moisturizers.

■ The easiest place to bathe a newborn is in a towel-lined sink or baby tub in a warm room.

■ Get all supplies ready. Turn on the answering machine or take your phone off the hook. Never leave an infant unattended for even an instant.

■ Run several inches of lukewarm water and test water temperature.

■ Put baby in the tub with your forearm supporting his head and neck.

■ If baby doesn't like to be completely naked, leave some clothes on and wash the body in sections.

- Wash baby from head to toe, getting between all the skin creases. Clean genitals last.

- Use a dampened cotton ball to wipe each eyelid from the inside corner out. Clean face, ears and scalp with a wet washcloth. (Never insert a cotton swab into a child's ear; just wipe the outer folds.)

- Wash a girl with a front-to-rear motion, cleaning the vaginal area before the rectum.

- The foreskin of an uncircumcised boy adheres to the penis; do not try to pull it back, simply wash the outside.

- Pat baby dry and cover his head to prevent a chill.

Safety Tips

• To avoid scalding baby, never add water directly from the faucet while baby is in the tub. Always turn hot water off first so the faucet doesn't remain hot.

• Bubble baths can irritate baby's skin and cause urinary tract inflammations in girls. Avoid completely during the first year and limit later on.

• Use hypoallergenic moisturizers or lotions. Products with fragrances, additives and parabens may irritate baby skin.

To warm liquid soap, shampoo and lotions, float bottles in the tub.

THE EXPERT: Nelson Lee Novick, M.D., associate clinical professor of dermatology, Mount Sinai School of Medicine, New York, and author of *Baby Skin* (Clarkson Potter, 1991).

The average newborn will be changed as many as a dozen times a day, so use the time to have fun, stimulate and bond with baby.

Changing baby

- Sing a diaper-changing song using baby's name.

- Give a mini-massage.

- Kiss or tickle baby from head to toe.

- Blow on baby's tummy.

- Install a mobile or mirror nearby or tape up a revolving gallery of pictures at baby's eye level.

- Talk about what you're doing, naming body parts.

- Attach a toy to the changing table with plastic links to keep baby's hands occupied, especially when you're applying diaper cream.

THE EXPERT: Riverside Mothers Group, authors of *Entertain Me* (Pocket Books, 1993).

Protect baby from diaper rash

■ Keep area dry and clean. Change diapers often.

■ Avoid plastic diaper covers.

■ After a bowel movement, gently wipe genitals with a soft cloth and water or a hypoallergenic moisturizer on a cotton ball. (Wipes may irritate a newborn's sensitive skin. Use alcohol-free wipes on older babies.)

■ Use a thin layer of diaper rash ointment like zinc oxide or a little cornstarch powder. (Powder with talc can be harmful if inhaled.)

■ Air is a great healer; occasionally leave baby bare-bottomed, but beware of puddles.

Diaper rash occurs when constant wetness and prolonged contact with the chemicals and bacteria in waste irritate baby's sensitive skin.

To avoid getting sprayed while changing an infant boy, cover his penis. Boys often urinate when cool air hits their naked bodies.

THE EXPERT: Nelson Lee Novick, M.D., associate clinical professor of dermatology, Mount Sinai School of Medicine, New York, and author of *Baby Skin* (Clarkson Potter, 1991).

Daily care tips

Belly button care

■ An infant's umbilical cord stump needs to be kept dry and clean until it falls off.

■ Clean the area several times a day with an alcohol-dipped cotton ball or cotton swab.

■ Fold diaper tops down below the stump to prevent irritation, or buy newborn diapers with a special cutout notch. Within two weeks, the cord will blacken, turn stiff and fall off. Call your pediatrician if the area reddens or oozes.

Cradle cap

■ Cradle cap is a patchy, scaly crust on the scalp. Apply mineral oil or baby lotion to soften; then comb out scales with a fine-toothed comb. For severe problems, your pediatrician may recommend a medicated shampoo.

Trimming tiny fingernails

■ A newborn's nails grow quickly. You may have to trim them several times a week.

■ Use a blunt-edged infant nail scissor or clipper.

■ Trim when baby is asleep or after a bath when nails are soft. Hold baby's hand so his fingers and yours point in the same direction. Cut nails straight across. Use a soft emery board on rough edges.

 THE EXPERT: National Association of Pediatric Nurse Associates and Practitioners.

What to pack in your diaper bag

The trick to keeping baby clean, fed, comfortable and stimulated on the go is a well-stocked diaper bag. Replace any supplies you've used immediately after each outing so your bag is ready to go any time you are.

What you need

- 3–5 diapers, wipes and diaper ointment

- Changing pad

- Bib and burp cloth

- Complete change of clothes for baby

- Hat and sweater

- An extra top for yourself

- Teethers, pacifier, toys, books

- Sunscreen (over 6 months)

- Snacks

- Add at the last minute: bottle of formula and/or water in an insulated pack and an extra nipple

- Zippered plastic bags (for dirty clothes, diapers, etc.)

In case of emergency: pack spare change for phone calls; a list of phone numbers and addresses for a local cab company, doctor, dentist, Mom's and Dad's offices, and any pertinent medical information you may need when you're away from home.

THE EXPERT: Heidi Murkoff, coauthor of *What to Expect When You're Expecting* (Workman, 1984), *What to Expect the First Year* (1989), and *What to Expect the Toddler Years* (1994).

Colic is an overused and misunderstood term often applied to normal infant fussiness. Although researchers still don't know what causes it, there are many theories and dozens of suggested remedies.

Coping with colic

■ Some doctors say it's a miscommunication between baby and parent or a developmental stage, while others blame an immature digestive track or say it results from an unusual sensitivity to stimulation.

■ Not every fussy baby has colic. Your baby may have a physical problem or a daily fussy period. A breast-fed baby may have a reaction like colic to dairy products or other foods in his mother's diet. If you are concerned about baby's behavior, consult your pediatrician.

■ If your baby is colicky, patience is the key to survival as you learn to cope with the frustration and exhaustion that come with the territory. Enlist the help of your spouse, relatives and friends to give you a needed break. Don't blame yourself. Don't look for a cure. Colic is usually outgrown by 3 or 4 months of age.

Soothing suggestions to try with any fussy baby:

■ Try the obvious: feed, burp, change and hold baby.

■ Offer a pacifier.

■ Swaddle baby in a soft, lightweight blanket.

■ Lay baby facedown across your knees and gently rub his back.

■ Walk with baby in a front carrier.

■ Rock baby in a swing, carriage, or cradle.

■ Dance holding baby close.

■ Sing or repeat a rhythmic chant while holding baby.

■ Give baby a relaxing, warm bath.

■ Calm baby with a massage.

The definition of colic is more than three hours a day of irritability, fussiness or crying, occurring more than three days a week, for longer than three weeks, in an otherwise healthy baby. Crying spells can occur around the clock but often become worse in the early evening. About 20 percent of babies behave this way.

 THE EXPERT: Dr. Marc Weissbluth, associate professor of pediatrics at Northwestern University Medical School, Chicago, and author of *Crybabies: Coping With Colic* (Berkley Books, 1984).

• The American Academy of Pediatrics recommends that healthy, full-term infants be placed on their backs or sides for sleep until they begin to roll over — between 4 and 7 months — to lower the risk of SIDS, Sudden Infant Death Syndrome (unexplained death of an apparently healthy infant).

• Always use a firm mattress — soft surfaces, like beanbags, pillows or waterbeds can suffocate an infant. Avoid heavy blankets or quilts that restrict baby's movements.

Sleep

Baby's sleep patterns

■ Don't expect regular sleep patterns from a newborn. By about 3 months baby should develop a regular 24-hour schedule with the longest period of sleep at night.

■ By 5 or 6 months, most babies no longer need to eat during the night.

■ Help baby develop good sleeping patterns by establishing a consistent routine of bedtime rituals — sleep, wake-up and naptimes — as well as play, feedings and bath.

■ After 5 months, don't make a habit of rocking, patting, singing or letting your infant fall asleep in your arms. Babies who learn to fall asleep by themselves have an easier time getting back to sleep by themselves when they awaken in the middle of the night.

For more information on SIDS and local support groups, call the Sudden Infant Death Syndrome Alliance: 800-221-SIDS.

The Ferber method

Although some people misunderstand it, this method does not consist of ignoring your baby's cries until he cries himself to sleep. Instead, it is a gradual technique in which you wait increasing intervals before going in to a crying baby. The baby eventually falls asleep on his own and after doing this several times, it starts to feel normal and expected.

Dr. Ferber points out that this method works best for children who have learned to associate something the parents do — rocking, patting, singing — with falling asleep. You can begin to use this method for babies over 5 months.

■ Put baby in his crib while he's awake. Leave the room.

■ If baby cries, wait five minutes before going back in. Stay only two to three minutes to verbally comfort him. Do not pick baby up.

■ If baby continues to cry, return to the room in 10 minutes and then in intervals of 15 minutes until he falls asleep.

■ Each subsequent night, increase the amount of time you wait before going in to baby — up to 15 minutes the first night and as long as 25 minutes after a few nights. Baby should learn to fall asleep on his own after several nights.

Help your child learn to fall asleep by himself with the "progressive waiting" technique.

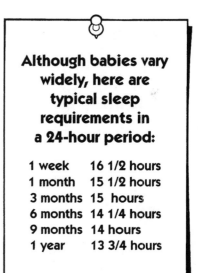

Although babies vary widely, here are typical sleep requirements in a 24-hour period:

1 week	16 1/2 hours
1 month	15 1/2 hours
3 months	15 hours
6 months	14 1/4 hours
9 months	14 hours
1 year	13 3/4 hours

THE EXPERT: Richard Ferber, M.D., director of the Center for Pediatric Sleep Disorders at Children's Hospital, Boston, and author of *Solve Your Child's Sleep Problems* (Fireside,1985).

Massage is a great way to bond with baby, show your love through touch, stimulate the senses, relieve gas, and relax you both. Begin touching baby right after birth with gentle caresses and build up to a full massage routine.

How to give an infant massage

- Keep fingernails short and smooth.

- Remove all jewelry.

- Lubricate hands with vegetable fruit oils (coconut, almond), which are safe if ingested.

- Rub hands together to warm. Show them to baby, asking: "Are you ready for your massage?" Watch for cues that mean "yes" — a calm, alert state and eye contact.

- Lie baby on his back (with a diaper under him) on a blanket, towel or sheepskin in a warm, draft-free room.

- Use slow, gentle, but firm movements with the balls of your fingers or palms. Feathery strokes can tickle. Start with a circular motion on the crown of the head and forehead.

As you stroke, watch baby's reactions to discover how and where he likes to be touched. If baby fusses when you massage one area, try another. Try different degrees of pressure and talk or sing softly while you massage.

- Move to the legs. Using the curve of your hand that makes a "C" between thumb and forefinger, stroke from hip to ankle, alternating hands on both the inside and outside of each leg. Use the pads of your thumb to massage baby's heels to the tip of each toe.

- Stroke abdomen in a clockwise motion, widening circles and ending at the lower left belly to help eliminate gas. Make a scooping motion from navel to pubic bone, using outside edge of each hand, one after the other.

- Roll baby on his stomach and massage the back of his head, neck and along the shoulders with a flat hand and long strokes. Place open hands on his back, alternating back-and-forth movements.

- Massage the arms and hands with the same strokes used on the legs.

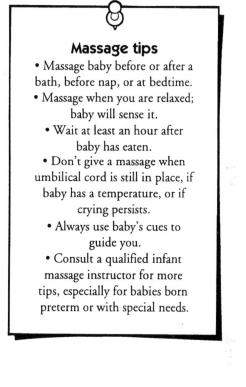

Massage tips
• Massage baby before or after a bath, before nap, or at bedtime.
• Massage when you are relaxed; baby will sense it.
• Wait at least an hour after baby has eaten.
• Don't give a massage when umbilical cord is still in place, if baby has a temperature, or if crying persists.
• Always use baby's cues to guide you.
• Consult a qualified infant massage instructor for more tips, especially for babies born preterm or with special needs.

For the name of a certified infant massage instructor in your area, call the International Association of Infant Massage: 800-248-5432.

THE EXPERT: International Association of Infant Massage.

Stain removal tips

Treat stains quickly, and don't put clothes in the dryer before stains are removed. If baby is sensitive to bleach or your detergent, switch brands or rinse well before drying.

Formula, juice, baby food	Rinse in cold water as soon as possible. Rub detergent into the stain or use a pretreating product and soak. Launder in hottest water safe for the fabric using an all-fabric or chlorine bleach.
Medicine, liquid vitamins, baby oil	Dampen and treat with detergent or pretreating product. Launder in warm water using chlorine bleach and extra detergent. If stain remains, sponge with cleaning fluid. Rinse and relaunder.
Urine or stool	Remove solids. Soak in warm water. Pretreat stain and launder in hottest water safe for fabric with appropriate bleach.
Vomit	Soak in cold water. Sponge stain with a solution of one quart ammonia and a half teaspoon of liquid detergent.

Washing cloth diapers

For best results, don't leave cloth diapers unwashed for more than 24 hours.

■ Remove solids and rinse.

■ Collect diapers in a pail containing a solution of water
mixed with either your own solution of borax, detergent, and one to
two tablespoons of chlorine bleach per gallon of water, or a special
diaper-soaking product.

■ Pour diapers and solution into
washer and set controls to spin.

■ Use detergent and warm water to presoak, or else
set washer on wash cycle and stop after agitation begins.

■ Wash on a regular cycle with hot water, detergent and diluted
chlorine bleach. Rinse in cold water.

■ Limit fabric softener; too much reduces absorbency. Dry diapers
on regular cycle.

 THE EXPERT: Maytag Consumer Education.

FEEDING

Although breast-feeding is natural, it is a learned process that may take time, advice and support. Don't despair.

Breast-feeding

■ Recognize and respond to baby's hunger cues. A newborn ready to nurse may root when held, turning toward you with lips puckered and mouth open.

■ Choose a private, calm setting.

■ Get into a comfortable position. Use pillows to avoid arm or back strain.

■ Position baby on his side with his whole body facing you. His head should be in line with the rest of his body and at breast level so he can easily reach your nipple.

■ Cup your breast with your free hand — fingers underneath, and thumb on the top — and guide it into baby's mouth.

- Help baby latch on properly. Tickle his lower lip with your nipple to stimulate his rooting reflex. Guide your nipple and some of your areola into baby's mouth. The tip of his nose should touch your breast. Make sure baby has room to breathe; you may have to hold down your breast.

- Make sure that both breasts get equal time. (Some doctors recommend nursing on both breasts at each feeding, while others advise using primarily one breast per feeding and alternating. Ask your pediatrician or lactation counselor.)

- If you use both breasts per feeding, start each feeding with the last breast nursed. (Switch a bracelet or pin from side to side to keep track.)

- Feed baby on demand for the first six weeks, while your milk supply is getting established. The more baby nurses, the more milk you produce.

- Let baby end the nursing rather than going by the clock, within reason.

For nursing information, mother-to-mother support, or a local lactation consultant, call International Lactation Consultant Association: 312-541-1710 or La Leche League International: 800-LA-LECHE.

THE EXPERT: La Leche League International.

You know baby is getting enough breast milk when he:

- Nurses frequently — every one and a half to three hours during the newborn period or about eight to 12 times daily.

- Has six to eight really wet diapers, and two to five stools daily, beginning the third day after birth.

- Gains four to seven ounces a week, or one pound a month.

- Grows in length and head circumference.

- Appears healthy, active and alert.

Breast-feeding facts

• The components of mother's breast milk continue to change to meet baby's needs. During the first few days after delivery breasts produce colostrum, containing many infection-fighting antibodies. Between the second and sixth day milk begins to come in.

• Even during the course of a feeding breast milk changes, starting off high in water and volume and becoming more fat-concentrated and calorie dense at the end.

• Wait until your milk supply is established — about five to six weeks after birth — to introduce an occasional bottle of breast milk or formula. Continue to nurse and express milk often to keep up your milk supply.

NEWBORN • Breast-feeding

Pumping and storing breast milk

■ Use clean four-ounce bottles each time you pump. Date each one.

■ Refrigerate and use within 48 to 72 hours. (Breast milk can be left at room temperature for six to eight hours, if you can't get to a refrigerator.)

■ For longer storage, refrigerate and then freeze in small amounts. Allow room for expansion.

■ Frozen breast milk can be stored for two weeks in the freezer section of a single-door refrigerator; four months in a separate-door freezer, and six months in a deep freezer.

■ If you store milk in plastic nurser bags, put several in a zippered freezer bag to prevent freezer burn.

Thawing breast milk

• Thaw frozen milk in the refrigerator overnight (and use within 48 hours), or hold container under warm water until it reaches room temperature.
• Do not thaw breast milk in a microwave; valuable nutrients may be destroyed.
• Breast milk separates; shake bottle before using.

THE EXPERT: La Leche League International.

49

The American Academy of Pediatrics advises that infants be fed iron-fortified formula for the first year of life. There are many brands and varieties to choose from. Ask your pediatrician to help you pick one based on your baby's needs.

Bottle-feeding

Preparing

■ Always wash your hands before preparing baby's bottle.

■ Sterilize bottles and nipples before their first use in a dishwasher or by immersing in boiling water for one minute. Ask your pediatrician whether he recommends resterilization before subsequent feedings. Many doctors say it is not necessary and you can simply wash bottles with hot, soapy water, rinse and air dry.

■ Never use a rusty, bulging or badly dented can of formula.

■ Refrigerate open cans and use within 48 hours.

■ Follow directions carefully. Powders and concentrates must be mixed with the correct amount of water.

■ Never leave a bottle of formula at room temperature for more than one hour. Discard formula if baby begins a bottle but doesn't finish it within the hour.

Serving

■ Never prop a bottle in baby's mouth; he could choke or take in too much air.

■ Hold baby in your arms, with his head higher than the rest of his body. Tip bottle so milk fills the nipple and insert into his mouth. If baby is getting too much air, try bottles with disposable plastic liners.

■ Experiment with different brands, sizes, and shapes of nipples and bottles to see what works for you and baby.

Bottle-fed newborns eat every three to four hours, taking two to three ounces per feeding, or 16 to 24 ounces a day. A 4- to 6-month-old will drink six to eight ounces four or five times a day, for a total of about 32 ounces daily.

THE EXPERT: Barney Softness, M.D., pediatrician; clinical instructor at Cornell University Medical College, New York, and a fellow with the American Academy of Pediatrics.

Although it's never been proven that babies prefer drinking their bottles warm, many parents prefer to offer them that way.

How to safely microwave bottles

You can warm bottles by heating them in a pot of water or by holding them under hot, running water. Many doctors advise against using the microwave, but if you decide to occasionally use one, do so safely.

- Use uncapped, clear plastic bottles; glass may crack and colored plastic bottles become too hot.

- Never use plastic bottle liners — they can explode. And don't microwave nipples.

- Heat only refrigerated formula or milk. Liquid at room temperature overheats easily and doesn't need warming.

- Do not microwave breast milk — valuable nutrients may be destroyed.

- Microwave at least four ounces of liquid (less can overheat) for no more than 30 seconds at full power; eight-ounce bottles for no more than 45 seconds.

- After heating and recapping, invert bottle several times to eliminate hot spots.

- Test formula by placing several drops on the back of your hand (more sensitive than the inner wrist). It should not feel hot.

THE EXPERT: Madeleine Sigman-Grant, Ph.D., R.D., assistant professor, Department of Food Sciences, Pennsylvania State University.

Burping basics

- To release gas trapped in baby's stomach, burp an infant after every few ounces of formula, or each time you switch breasts if you're nursing. Don't interrupt a baby who's contentedly feeding; sometimes just changing baby's position helps.

- Pat baby's back in an upward motion while you hold him with his head on your shoulder; sit him up on your lap, supporting his chest and head with one hand; or lie him facedown on your lap.

- Keep a cloth over your shoulder or under baby's chin in case he spits up.

- Hold a bottle-fed baby at a 45-degree angle to feed or use collapsible bottle liners so he'll swallow less air.

Hiccups are common in young babies. They usually don't bother them and tend to stop shortly on their own. A few sips from a water bottle may help. If hiccups occur during a feeding, try to burp baby. Wait for them to subside before you resume feeding.

THE EXPERT: National Association of Pediatric Nurse Associates and Practitioners.

HEALTH

What should be in every parent's medicine cabinet

A well-stocked medicine cabinet can be a lifesaver. Regularly discard outdated pills and vitamins by flushing them down the toilet; keep all medications in their original containers, and keep your entire cabinet off-limits to children.

What you need

- Rectal and oral thermometers

- Petroleum jelly

- Syrup of ipecac

- Cotton swabs and cotton balls

- Liquid acetaminophen

- Plastic bandages; sterile gauze squares; adhesive tape

- Blunt scissors; tweezers

- Medicine cup, spoon or dropper

- Rubbing alcohol

- Antibiotic and hydrocortisone creams

- Saline nose drops; nasal aspirator

- Sunscreen SPF 15 or higher

- Elastic support bandage

THE EXPERT: American Academy of Pediatrics.

When to call the doctor

Ask your pediatrician about symptoms of common illnesses your baby is likely to experience, how to treat them, and when to call the doctor or go straight to an emergency room.

Remember: if you're ever concerned about your baby's health — no matter what time of night or day — call your pediatrician and err on the side of caution. Early detection and treatment of many conditions depend on a parent's observation of changes in their baby's behavior and appearance.

Call immediately if your infant exhibits any of these symptoms:

- Poor appetite or difficulty sucking

- Lethargy or difficulty being awakened

- Weak, mousy cry or high-pitched whimpering or moaning

- Constant crying or excessive irritability

- Pain or tenderness in any area

- No urination for eight to 12 hours

- Sunken eyes or doughy skin that doesn't return to normal when pressed

- Any elevation of temperature in a baby 3 months or younger; a rectal temperature of 100.5 degrees Fahrenheit or higher in a baby between 3 and 6 months

---

THE EXPERT: Donald Schiff, M.D., pediatrician; past president of the American Academy of Pediatrics and professor of pediatrics at the University of Colorado Medical School, Denver.

Taking temperature

The most reliable way to take an infant's temperature is with a rectal thermometer — either a mercury or digital version. Although electronic ear thermometers are not as accurate with babies under 1 year, they are much easier and less stressful for the parents.

To take a rectal reading

■ Hold the nonsilver end of a rectal mercury thermometer and shake until the mercury band is below the 96-degree mark. (If using a digital thermometer, follow the manufacturer's instructions.)

■ Place baby facedown across your lap, or on a firm, flat surface.

■ Dip bulb in petroleum jelly.

■ Gently spread baby's buttocks and slide bulb into rectum no more than half an inch.

■ Hold thermometer in place for one to two minutes between your index and middle fingers, using your other fingers to keep the baby's buttocks from moving.

■ Remove and read temperature where silver line stops.

■ Before putting away, shake thermometer down and wash with soap and cool water. Wipe with rubbing alcohol. Discard, if you notice even a tiny crack.

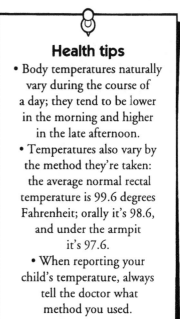

Health tips

• Body temperatures naturally vary during the course of a day; they tend to be lower in the morning and higher in the late afternoon.

• Temperatures also vary by the method they're taken: the average normal rectal temperature is 99.6 degrees Fahrenheit; orally it's 98.6, and under the armpit it's 97.6.

• When reporting your child's temperature, always tell the doctor what method you used.

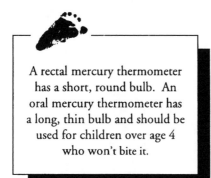

A rectal mercury thermometer has a short, round bulb. An oral mercury thermometer has a long, thin bulb and should be used for children over age 4 who won't bite it.

THE EXPERT: National Association of Pediatric Nurse Associates and Practitioners.

Routine vision checks should be part of every visit to the pediatrician to detect any problems.

How to spot a vision problem

Infants can see from birth, although their vision is likely to be blurry and won't develop fully for several months.

Notify your pediatrician if you notice any of the following warning signs:

■ After 2 months of age, one eye wanders or eyes are crossed.

■ When gazing at something intently, only one eye appears to be aimed at the object.

■ Baby frequently squints or tilts head to one side when examining something.

■ Baby doesn't appear to see or react to a family member approaching from a distance.

☞ THE EXPERT: American Optometric Association.

How to spot a hearing problem

Long before your infant is able to say a word, he can understand what you're saying to him. Even a newborn will turn his head toward the familiar sound of his parents' voices or be startled by a loud noise.

Your child's hearing is critical to his speech and language development, so the earlier any problems are detected and diagnosed, the better.

Have your child evaluated by a specialist if, in the first 6 months, he:

- Does not awaken, startle, move, cry or react to unexpected loud noises.

- Does not freely imitate sound.

- Cannot be soothed by voice alone.

- Does not turn his head in the direction of a voice.

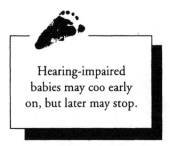

Hearing-impaired babies may coo early on, but later may stop.

THE EXPERT: American Academy of Otolaryngology — Head and Neck Surgery, Inc.

SAFETY

Car seats are required by law in every state. Always be sure that your baby is properly secured in the seat and that the seat is properly attached to the car. Never start your car until everyone is buckled in.

Car seat safety

- Read and follow manufacturer instructions and examine your car owner's manual before anchoring a car seat.

- The safest place for any age child is in the middle of the backseat.

- Once in place, check the car seat by pushing it forward and from side to side. If it moves or the belt loosens, move the seat to another spot in the car; try a different car seat, or take additional steps to make it secure. Contact the seat manufacturer or SafetyBeltSafe U.S.A. for technical advice.

- When using a lap/shoulder belt, make sure the belt locks into place. If not, check the car manual about how to add a locking clip.

To keep a rear-facing infant happy, tape a photo of Mom and Dad or a rotating gallery of black-and-white or primary-colored pictures to the seat back for baby to look at.

- From birth to 1 year and up to 20 pounds, infants should be in a rear-facing car seat.

- Never use a rear-facing car seat in a seat equipped with an airbag.

- If an infant's head flops forward, put a tightly rolled towel under the front edge of the car seat to tilt it back slightly.

- More important than the weight recommendation is whether your baby's head is higher than the back of the seat; if that happens, it's time to buy a larger car seat for proper protection.

For a large baby who weighs more than 20 pounds before his first birthday, there is at least one convertible car seat on the market that can be used for up to 32 pounds rear-facing and up to 40 pounds forward-facing. Call Safeline Children's Products Co.: 800-829-1625 and ask about the Sit'n'Stroll

THE EXPERT: SafetyBeltSafe U.S.A.

LEARNING

Babies don't need to be taught how to talk, but there are ways to promote language development.

Help baby build word power

- Talk, sing and read to baby from birth.

- Repeat baby's coos and babbles. Speak as if you're having a dialogue; pause after you ask a question to let baby respond.

- Engage baby's attention: make eye contact and address him by name when talking or singing to him.

- Make up silly songs and rhymes with baby's name.

- Talk about what you're doing and what you see, hear and smell: "Let's put cream on." "I smell cookies."

- Converse at increasingly complex levels. Babies understand more than you may think they do.

Baby talk timetable

BIRTH-1 MONTH
Baby gurgles, makes noises, and cries in a way that may not seem to vary in intensity or pitch.

1-3 MONTHS
Begins to make cooing "ooh" sounds by moving air through the front of the mouth.

4-6 MONTHS
Babbles, laughs and chuckles. Begins to engage in real give-and-take communication.

6-9 MONTHS
Repeats sounds made by parents. Changes pitch and inflection, making babbling sounds like speech. Begins to use the lips and tongue to produce repetitive consonant sounds like "dadada" or "lalala." ("Dada" often comes before "mama" because it's easier to say.)

9-12 MONTHS
May say first recognizable word.

THE EXPERT: Naomi Baron, Ph.D., professor of linguistics at American University, Washington, D.C., and author of *Growing Up With Language: How Children Learn to Talk* (Addison-Wesley, 1993).

PLAYING

Toy box favorites Birth-1 year

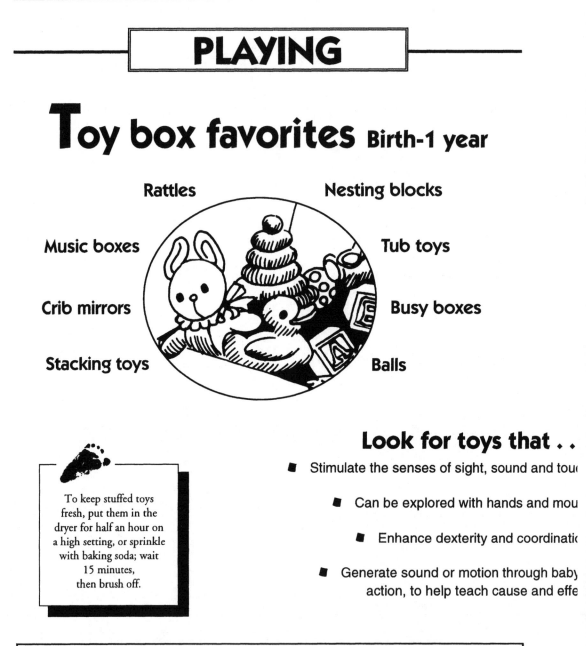

Rattles

Music boxes

Crib mirrors

Stacking toys

Nesting blocks

Tub toys

Busy boxes

Balls

Look for toys that . .

■ Stimulate the senses of sight, sound and tou...

■ Can be explored with hands and mou...

■ Enhance dexterity and coordinati...

■ Generate sound or motion through baby...
   action, to help teach cause and effe...

To keep stuffed toys fresh, put them in the dryer for half an hour on a high setting, or sprinkle with baking soda; wait 15 minutes, then brush off.

THE EXPERT: Helen Boehm, Ph.D., educational psychologist and toy expert, senior vice president at the MTV Network, and author of *The Right Toys* (Bantam Books, 1986).

Playing with baby

Most of the best games for baby require no special gadgets — just a penchant for play.

Many experts say that parents are a child's first and most influential teachers. Help your baby learn from the start with simple games that engage him and stimulate his senses. You'll both have fun and bond with each other while baby picks up such skills as communication, body awareness, and much more.

- Peekaboo: Cover your face with your hands or a blanket and quickly uncover it. This shows baby that something exists even when it cannot be seen and helps him prepare for separations from you.

- Pat-a-cake: As you tickle baby's tummy and roll his hands to form the cake, he begins to get a sense of his body, of himself as a separate person, and of his intimate relationship with you.

- Monkey see, monkey do: Put your face about 10 inches from baby's; smile, laugh, stick out your tongue, or open your mouth wide and freeze your expression. Soon he'll imitate you.

- Can you reach? To encourage a baby discovering mobility, place appealing objects slightly out of reach. Help baby get them by gently pushing him forward on the soles of his feet.

- Do you hear what I hear? Make baby aware of his surroundings by talking about what you see, hear and feel. Let him touch the bark of a tree; smell freshly baked cookies; show him how his body makes shadows, and help him listen to birds singing.

Make early games tactile, rhythmic, repetitive and fun.

THE EXPERT: Mildred Winter, early childhood educator and executive director of Parents as Teachers National Center.

Chapter Three

OLDER BABY
SIX MONTHS–ONE YEAR

FEEDING

There's no universal right time to wean baby from breast to bottle or cup. Ideally it will be a natural process as an older baby loses interest.

Weaning

You may have to wean baby twice, at less than 6 months from breast to bottle, and at approximately 1 1/2 years from bottle to cup. If you nurse longer you can skip the bottle altogether. Wean nursing baby gradually to help both Mom and baby adjust physically and emotionally.

◆ Let someone other than Mom give baby her first bottles. Avoid routines or places (like rocking chair) associated with nursing.

◆ Offer a bottle at the time baby has the least interest in the comfort aspects of nursing and is simply hungry — like lunchtime. (The last nursings to go are usually the "snuggle-time" ones, upon waking and right before bed.)

◆ Substitute a bottle at one feeding for several days; then gradually increase the number of bottles as your breasts adapt and it feels comfortable.

◆ Provide extra attention, like holding and cuddling baby, so she doesn't associate the withdrawal of nursing with the withdrawal of affection.

After 6 months, infants need no more than a quart of formula a day because solid foods supply additional calories and nutrients. The American Academy of Pediatrics recommends switching to whole cow's milk after 12 months, when baby's stomach matures. At age 2, you can switch to low-fat or skim milk.

THE EXPERT: International Lactation Consultant Association.

The American Academy of Pediatrics recommends that babies begin solid foods by 4 to 6 months, with a gradual introduction of one food at a time. This gives babies the chance to get used to each taste and helps parents note any adverse reactions.

Feeding solids

◆ Give baby a single-ingredient food and wait three to five days before trying another. Check for allergic reactions including rash, diarrhea, wheezing or vomiting. If symptoms appear, eliminate the suspected food and talk to your pediatrician.

◆ Introduce new foods at breakfast or lunch, not dinner; then, if something doesn't agree with baby you can deal with the problem during the day, and you and baby will avoid a sleepless night.

◆ Start with a teaspoon or two of iron-fortified rice cereal (try oatmeal and barley next), mixed to a soupy consistency with breast milk or formula.

◆ Gradually increase serving size.

◆ Once baby has accepted cereal, begin introducing other foods with the "round robin" approach: add a fruit, then a vegetable, and then a new cereal (save wheat, the most allergenic grain, for last). Don't go through all the sweet fruits first or baby may not want to try any veggies.

◆ Increase texture as baby gets the hang of it.

◆ As a general rule, introduce yellow-hued fruits and vegetables first (Golden Delicious apples), orange ones next (sweet potatoes), and dark green and red ones last (broccoli and beets). (Citrus fruits, melons and corn are the exception to the yellow-orange rule and should be introduced only after 10 months.)

These companies operate toll-free hotlines to answer questions about commercial baby food:
Gerber: 800-4-GERBER
Beech-Nut: 800-523-6633
Earth's Best: 800-442-4221

THE EXPERT: Martha and David Kimmel, food consultants and authors of *Mommy Made and Daddy Too! Home Cooking for a Healthy Baby & Toddler* (Bantam Books, 1990).

When to introduce what foods

Birth to 6 months	• *Breast milk or formula*
6 months	• *Rice and oat cereals* • *Banana (very ripe), applesauce, acorn squash, butternut squash, sweet potato, apple juice*
7 months	• *Barley and wheat cereals* • *Peaches, plums, carrots, peas, green beans*
8 months	• *Kasha, brown rice, bread* • *Apricots, zucchini, summer squash* • *Chicken, turkey* • *Plain yogurt*

9 months	• *Oat cereal circles, teething biscuits* • *Papaya, avocado, asparagus* • *Lean beef* • *Cream cheese, cottage cheese, ricotta*
10 months	• *Egg-free pasta* • *Citrus fruits, nectarines, prunes, beets, broccoli* • *Lamb, liver* • *Mild cheeses (cheddar, mozzarella, Muenster, Monterey Jack, Swiss)*
11 months	• *Kiwi, spinach, baked white potato, parsnips* • *Veal, egg yolks* • *Combination purees (chicken-vegetable, beef-noodle)*
12 months	• *Cantaloupe, watermelon, blueberries, cauliflower, cucumber, artichoke (pureed heart), eggplant* • *Tofu, lentils, lima beans, dried peas and beans* • *White-fleshed fish, pork*

 THE EXPERT: Martha and David Kimmel, food consultants and authors of *Mommy Made and Daddy Too! Home Cooking for a Healthy Baby & Toddler* (Bantam Books, 1990).

Your own baby food can be fresher, healthier, less expensive and taste better than many store bought brands. Plus, you know exactly what baby's getting.

Homemade baby food

◆ Cook all food before pureeing (except ripe bananas and avocados) to make them more digestible.

◆ Wash, peel, pit, and seed fruits and vegetables. Cook promptly to preserve nutrients.

◆ Use blender, food processor or food mill to process until smooth.

◆ Thin baby's first meals with breast milk, formula or water. Later, add chicken, beef stock or steaming juices.

◆ When baby begins to gum or chew, thicken food with rice cereal, mashed potatoes or arrowroot starch.

◆ Use yogurt to cool and smooth pureed fruits and vegetables.

Storing

◆ Homemade food will last three days in the refrigerator and one month in the freezer. Do not refreeze defrosted food.

◆ For beginning eaters, freeze tablespoon-sized dollops of pureed foods on a wax paper-lined baking sheet. Once solid, peel off and store in freezer bags. Or freeze pureed food in ice cube trays or baby food jars, leaving room for expansion.

◆ Date all foods.

Serving

◆ Defrost frozen food in the refrigerator, heat uncovered jars in a small saucepan of water, or microwave briefly (mix thoroughly and test before serving).

◆ Never feed baby directly from storage jars; bacteria in saliva will spoil any leftover food.

◆ Discard food left standing at room temperature for more than one hour; less in hot weather.

Finger foods
Once baby can feed herself, offer an assortment of finger foods — big enough for her to pick up, but small enough to prevent choking.
• Steamed wedges of apple, pear, carrot, zucchini and squash
• Steamed asparagus spears
• Ripe banana and avocado spears
• Semisoft cheese cubes
• Gelatin cubes
• Egg-free pasta
• Oat cereal circles (like Cheerios)

THE EXPERT: Martha and David Kimmel, food consultants and authors of *Mommy Made and Daddy Too! Home Cooking for a Healthy Baby & Toddler* (Bantam Books, 1990).

Avoidance of an allergenic food is the only way to prevent an allergic reaction. Some foods may be reintroduced in the future under a doctor's supervision.

Food allergies

Food allergies are common in infants and children. Symptoms can range from mild to life-threatening and include vomiting, diarrhea, hives, coughing, congestion, eczema, runny nose, watery or itching eyes, and swelling of lips and throat.

Reactions can occur within minutes to several hours after eating the culprit food.

If your child exhibits any of these symptoms, talk to your pediatrician. If there is a severe reaction, like difficulty breathing, get medical help immediately.
If your child has a food allergy:

◆ Ask your doctor how to replace necessary nutrients.

◆ Always read ingredients carefully — manufacturers sometimes change them.

◆ If ingredient listings are unavailable, don't let your child eat the food.

◆ Know the scientific and technical names for the foods your child is allergic to — eggs may be listed as albumin or vitelline; wheat is in malt and graham flour.

◆ If your child has had a severe reaction, keep prescribed medication available at all times.

◆ Advise friends, teachers and caregivers about your child's allergies and what to do in case of a reaction. Provide a list of foods and ingredients to avoid.

◆ As your child gets older, make sure she won't be excluded from school picnics, birthdays and holiday parties by supplying her own "safe" foods.

The most common allergy-causing foods are milk, eggs, peanuts, soy and wheat products, nuts, fish and shellfish. Many food allergies are outgrown, although allergies to peanuts, nuts, fish and shellfish are usually lifelong.

Wait until baby's first birthday to serve honey; it may contain bacterial spores that can cause botulism in young children.

THE EXPERT: The Food Allergy Network.

There are two types of milk-related conditions: lactose intolerance — which is most common in adults and often gets worse with age — and milk allergies — usually seen in children and eventually outgrown.

Milk allergies

Lactose intolerance is caused by the lack of an enzyme needed to digest dairy products and can cause cramping, diarrhea and bloating. A milk allergy may cause wheezing, vomiting, hives and a stuffed nose. If your child has a severe reaction, like difficulty breathing, get medical help immediately.

◆ If you suspect your child has one of these conditions, consult your pediatrician before switching formulas or restricting diet. (Many infants are also allergic to soy and they may need a special hypoallergenic formula.)

◆ Check food labels for ingredients like casein, lactose and whey — all are milk products.

◆ If your child continues to have reactions once you think you've eliminated all milk products, look further; some medications contain lactose as filler, and deli meats may also contain milk products.

Cooking tips for a milk-free diet

◆ Use fruit juice instead of milk in dry cereal.

◆ Add applesauce to hot cereal.

◆ Blend a banana and some water until smooth and pour over cereal. (It looks like milk.)

◆ In baking, for one cup milk, substitute one cup water or one cup fruit juice plus one tablespoon oil or shortening.

Kosher symbols

Kosher symbols can make it easier to shop for a child on a milk-free diet. Because kosher kitchens never mix milk and meat, codes on some products indicate whether a product is milk free or whether it contains dairy products. (Continue to read ingredients to be certain a product is milk free.)

The word "Pareve" on a food label indicates that no milk is present in the product. A "D" listed next to the symbol for the kosher agency that checked the product ("K" or "U" in a circle) means the product contains milk. A "D" on a product that does not list milk in the ingredients may indicate the food was contaminated by milk during processing.

THE EXPERT: The Food Allergy Network.

HEALTH

When to call the doctor

◆ Temperature over 102 degrees
Fahrenheit

◆ Fever that lasts longer than
three days; a cold that doesn't
improve in a week

◆ Unusually pale, gray or
ashen complexion

◆ Limpness, lack of strength or
decreased movement of the limbs

◆ Poor coordination, staggering,
confusion

◆ Difficulty breathing; labored
or rapid breathing

◆ Persistent cough or cough that
occurs only at night

◆ Sunken eyeballs, dry mouth, loss
of skin elasticity

◆ Vacant expression or lack of
eye contact

◆ Crying and pulling on the ears
or ear discharge

◆ Prolonged diarrhea or
frequent vomiting

◆ Blood in stools or urine

Before you make a call, have all the
information your pediatrician may need.
If your child was with a caregiver or at day
care all day, find out from them whether
your child had a fever. Did she vomit?
What was her activity level? How was her
appetite? etc.

THE EXPERT: Donald Schiff, M.D., pediatrician; past president of the American Academy of Pediatrics and professor of pediatrics at the University of Colorado Medical School, Denver.

Fever

Fevers scare parents more than they hurt children. A fever is usually a sign that the body is fighting infection.

◆ Call the doctor when a baby older than 6 months has a temperature over 102 degrees Fahrenheit.

◆ Give acetaminophen (dosage by weight, not age). Never give aspirin — it's been associated with a serious condition called Reye's syndrome.

◆ Dress baby in light clothing.

◆ Encourage her to drink extra fluids — water or diluted fruit juice.

◆ Sponge baby — place her in a bath filled with one to two inches of tepid water — especially if her temperature is over 104 degrees Fahrenheit. Never cool her off with cold water or alcohol.

Taking temperature under the arm

Take temperature rectally until your child resists. If your baby is too squirmy to hold still, try an underarm reading; it's less accurate but easier.

• Hold the nonsilver end of either a rectal or oral thermometer and shake until the mercury band is below the 96-degree mark.

• Place the bulb end of the thermometer in the middle of your child's bare, dry armpit. Hold her arm gently but firmly against her body for two to three minutes.

THE EXPERT: National Association of Pediatric Nurse Associates.

Teething symptoms may precede the appearance of a new tooth by several months. Drooling is one sign that the process has begun.

The American Academy of Pediatrics recommends a first trip to the dentist when your child is between the ages of 2 and 3 and has all 20 primary teeth.

Teething

Not all babies are bothered by teething, but those who are may become irritable and have decreased appetite and difficulty sleeping. Gums may swell and be tender. To soothe baby:

◆ Gently massage inflamed gums with a finger or cool, wet washcloth.

◆ Give baby something to chew on: teething biscuits or plastic teething rings. (Refrigerate water-filled ones; they can injure gums if frozen.)

◆ Try an over-the-counter product to ease soreness.

◆ Family remedies may suggest rubbing bourbon on sore gums, but doctors advise against any alcohol for babies.

Dental care

◆ Wipe an infant's gums with a piece of gauze after each feeding, at bedtime and after giving medicine (which may contain sugar).

◆ Never let baby fall asleep with a bottle of juice, formula or breast or cow's milk in her mouth. Extended exposure to the sugar in these liquids can cause developing teeth to discolor and decay.

◆ Once teeth erupt, begin brushing with a child-sized, soft-bristled brush and a pea-sized amount of toothpaste.

Teeth begin forming in utero and all 20 primary teeth are present in the jawbones at birth. Teeth usually begin to appear by 6 months and by age 3 your child should have all 20.

Here's the usual time frame and order for baby's teeth to arrive:

6-10 months
Lower two
front incisors

8-12 months
Top four incisors

10-16 months
Two more lower
front incisors

13-19 months
First-year molars

16-22 months
Pointed canines

23-33 months
Second-year molars

THE EXPERT: *American Academy of Pediatric Dentistry.*

Ears

How to spot a hearing problem

Have a baby between 6 and 12 months evaluated by a specialist if she:

◆ Does not point to familiar persons or objects when asked.

◆ Does not babble, or babbling has stopped.

◆ Does not understand simple phrases like "wave bye-bye" or "clap hands" by 12 months.

Ears and flying

• Children shouldn't fly in the early stages of an ear infection when the eustachian tube — which connects the nose and middle ear — is blocked. If there is a rapid change in air pressure, the already inflamed eardrum may retract or expand, causing sharp pain and possibly even rupture.

• Your pediatrician may suggest waiting three to five days after the start of antibiotics before flying and using a nasal spray or drops before takeoff if congestion remains.

• Even healthy children may experience discomfort during pressure changes, primarily during turbulence and landing. Nurse baby or give her a bottle, sippy cup or pacifier. Even crying helps equalize the pressure.

THE EXPERT: American Academy of Otolaryngology — Head and Neck Surgery, Inc.

Choking
(under age 1)

If your child is choking, but can still breathe, speak or cough, call your doctor for further advice before doing anything.

First aid for choking is necessary only if the child's airway is blocked so completely that she cannot cry, cough, breathe or speak, or is coughing weakly or making high-pitched sounds. In that case, do the following:

◆ Hold baby facedown resting on your forearm; support her head and keep it lower than chest.

◆ Give up to five rapid back blows with the heel of your hand between baby's shoulder blades.

◆ If obstruction remains, turn baby faceup and give up to five chest thrusts near the center of the breastbone using your middle and index fingers.

◆ Lift jaw and tongue — if you see a foreign object, sweep it out with your finger; do not poke blindly.

THE EXPERT: American Red Cross.

SAFETY

Remember the golden rule of child safety: "If it's there, your child will find it. If it can be done, your child will do it."

Childproofing your home

Begin childproofing by the time baby is 6 months old and can roll, crawl or move toward danger. Get down on your hands and knees and survey your home from a child's-eye view. Periodically reevaluate safety precautions as your child develops new abilities and reaches new stages. And always stay alert and supervise your child.

Bedroom

◆ Be sure hanging pictures and objects on dressers or bookshelves near crib are out of reach.

◆ Keep all "climbing" furniture away from windows.

◆ Use safety latches to keep drawers shut.

◆ Keep diaper pail securely closed.

◆ Install window guards or locks that allow windows to open only slightly.

◆ In parent's bedroom: don't empty pockets of coins, paper clips, pens, etc., and leave them where baby can reach. Keep closet doors closed.

Find out the risks associated with chemicals being used in and around your home; call the National Pesticide Telecommunications Network: 800-858-PEST.

Dining room

◆ Use placemats instead of tablecloths.

◆ Put knives on table only after adults are seated.

◆ Lock china cabinets.

Living room/den

◆ Bolt bookshelves and cabinets to walls.

◆ Put knickknacks out of reach.

◆ Keep VCR in a locked cabinet or use a VCR lock.

◆ Use a fireplace screen. Keep fireplace tools and matches off-limits.

◆ Remove glass tables.

◆ Cushion sharp table edges with corner guards or use safety bumpers.

◆ Examine furniture for exposed or loose nails, staples and upholstery buttons.

◆ Immediately remove ashtrays, wineglasses and dishes of mints or nuts after entertaining.

◆ Never leave lamp sockets empty. Screw bulbs in tightly.

 THE EXPERT: Jeanne Miller, childproofing expert, president of Perfectly Safe, and author of *The Perfectly Safe Home* (Fireside, 1991).

Kitchen

◆ Keep garbage in a latched pail or cabinet.

◆ When discarding plastic bags, fold lengthwise and tie several tight knots.

◆ Install a safety lock switch on garbage disposals.

◆ Cook on back burners. Turn pot handles toward the rear of the stove.

◆ Install stove knob covers or remove knobs.

◆ Keep a multipurpose fire extinguisher handy.

◆ Use childproof latches on cabinets containing cleansers, glassware, knives, electric appliances, and boxes of foil and plastic wrap with sharp edges.

◆ Keep dishwasher door latched.

Beware danger times when most accidents occur: early morning before parents are up, and late in the day when they're rushed or busy. Saturday, 3–6 P.M. is the worst accident time.

◆ Position high chair away from furniture or walls that can be used to push off from. Make sure appliance cords and items on countertops are out of reach.

◆ Don't let phone cord dangle where baby can reach.

Bathroom

◆ Keep bathroom door closed when not in use. Use safety knob covers.

◆ Set water heater thermostat to 120 degrees Fahrenheit or install an antiscald device.

◆ Put nonskid rubber mats in tub and shower.

◆ Use padded faucet protectors in the tub.

◆ Use plastic bottles and cups, not glass.

◆ Install toilet seat latch.

◆ Avoid automatic toilet cleaners that color water and may attract children.

◆ Lock up razors, cleansers, cosmetics, medicines, vitamins, perfume, aftershave and mouthwash.

◆ Unplug electric appliances and store out of reach.

◆ Install a ground fault circuit interrupter to prevent electrical shocks.

THE EXPERT: Jeanne Miller, childproofing expert, president of Perfectly Safe, and author of *The Perfectly Safe Home* (Fireside, 1991).

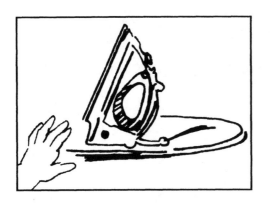

Basement and garage

◆ When ironing, make sure baby can't reach the ironing board or the iron cord. Safely store them away between uses.

◆ To prevent accidental drowning, never leave large buckets of liquid around.

◆ Lock up paint, antifreeze and pesticides.

◆ Lock up hardware, tools, rakes, lawn mowers and snowblowers. Teach children these are not toys.

◆ Store power tools unplugged.

◆ Keep washer and dryer lids closed and secured with safety latches.

◆ Make sure automatic garage door retracts if it touches anything before reaching the ground. Install switch out of child's reach or cover with a safety lock.

To hire a professional childproofer, look in your local yellow pages under "Safety Consultants." The following free catalogs offer childproofing equipment:
Perfectly Safe: 800-837-KIDS
The Safety Zone: 800-999-3030
Safety 1st: 800-962-7233

General household safety hints

◆ Install smoke detectors on every floor, especially outside bedrooms. (A typical two-story home needs a minimum of seven smoke detectors.) Test regularly and replace batteries twice a year when resetting clocks.

◆ Install electric outlet covers.

◆ Use cord shorteners on wires and blind cords.

◆ Rugs should have nonslip backs or pads underneath.

◆ Use nonpressure gates at top and bottom of stairs. (These are usually attached to the wall and more secure than pressure gates that can loosen if leaned against.)

◆ Remove or disengage door locks that can be locked from the inside without access from the outside.

◆ Keep doors from closing on fingers — keep a towel draped over the top.

◆ Keep litter box and pet food out of reach.

◆ Keep exercise equipment with movable parts off-limits.

◆ Always store hazardous products in their original marked containers and keep out of reach.

◆ Make sure visitors don't leave pocketbooks accessible to children; they may contain medicine, coins and paper clips a curious child could swallow.

 THE EXPERT: Jeanne Miller, childproofing expert, president of Perfectly Safe, and author of *The Perfectly Safe Home* (Fireside, 1991).

Childproofing your hotel room

◆ Make sure the room and building have fire and smoke alarms. Locate fire exits.

◆ Check carpets and couch cushions for small objects.

◆ Keep toiletries off-limits.

◆ Drape a towel over the bathroom door to prevent children from getting locked in.

◆ Remove glasses, ashtrays, matches and plants.

◆ Cushion or rearrange furniture with sharp edges.

◆ Keep windows and sliding glass doors locked and drapery and electrical cords out of reach.

◆ Never allow unsupervised children on a balcony.

◆ Block floor-level heating units from little fingers.

◆ Keep suitcases out of the way to prevent falls.

Some hotels, including Embassy Suites: 800-362-2779, and Ritz-Carlton Hotels: 800-241-3333, offer professionally childproofed rooms or childproofing kits. Check individual hotels for availability.

What you need in your travel/first aid/safety kit

◆ Medical insurance card

◆ Acetaminophen (like children's Tylenol)

◆ Dosage cup, spoon or dropper

◆ Plastic bandages

◆ Sunscreen and insect repellent

◆ Antibiotic ointment

◆ Syrup of ipecac

◆ Electrical outlet covers or electrical tape to cover outlets and tape down wires

◆ Night-light

◆ Phone numbers for your pediatrician and pharmacy

◆ Copy of any prescription your child regularly uses

When you arrive at your hotel, look up the number for the local Poison Control Center and locate the nearest emergency medical facility. For an extended visit, get the phone number of a local pediatrician.

THE EXPERT: Karl Neumann, M.D., New York City pediatrician and editor of *Traveling Healthy* newsletter.

Many common plants and flowers can be deadly to children when chewed, swallowed or rubbed on the skin. Reactions may range from a mild skin rash or stomach cramps to irregular heartbeat, convulsions and coma.

Plant safety

If you suspect that your child may have ingested a poisonous plant or one you're not sure of, call your local Poison Control Center immediately. (The following lists are not all-inclusive.)

Poisonous plants

- Azalea
- Buttercup
- Climbing nightshade
- Daffodil
- Dumbcane
- English ivy
- Hyacinth
- Hydrangea

- Iris
- Morning glory
- Philodendron
- Pokeweed
- Pothos
- Rhododendron
- Rubber plant
- Yew

Nonpoisonous plants

- African violet
- Aloe
- Bamboo palm
- Begonia
- Christmas cactus
- Daisy
- Dandelion
- Day Lily

- Dogwood
- Geranium
- Impatiens
- Jade
- Marigold
- Rose
- Spider
- Wax plant

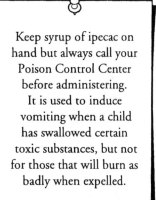

Keep syrup of ipecac on hand but always call your Poison Control Center before administering. It is used to induce vomiting when a child has swallowed certain toxic substances, but not for those that will burn as badly when expelled.

Beware dangerous holiday plants: holly and mistletoe berries are poisonous; poinsettia can cause skin irritations and gastrointestinal distress.

THE EXPERT: American Association of Poison Control Centers.

Lesser-known poisons

If you suspect your child has swallowed any of these substances, call your local Poison Control Center. Administer syrup of ipecac only if advised.

Mouthwash	Children are attracted by the color, smell and taste, but many brands contain more alcohol than beer or wine. One ounce of a high-alcohol mouthwash can cause seizures, brain damage, coma and death. Look for alcohol-free brands.
Aftershave and perfume	Several mouthfuls of cologne — which contain up to 90 percent alcohol — can cause drowsiness or even coma.
Iron pills and vitamins	The leading cause of poisoning death in children is the ingestion of adult-strength iron pills and prenatal vitamins with iron. A handful can be fatal. Even several children's chewable vitamins with iron can sicken a child.
Nicotine	Eating one cigarette, several butts, a handful of chewing tobacco, or half a piece of nicotine gum can cause vomiting, high blood pressure, irregular heartbeat, breathing difficulty and seizures in a child.
Mothballs	Children can mistake mothballs for candy. Ingestion can cause abdominal pain, vomiting, diarrhea, fever, seizures or coma.

Common hazardous household items

- ◆ Antifreeze and windshield washer fluid

- ◆ Cosmetics and nail products containing alcohol

- ◆ Drain opener

- ◆ Flavoring extracts like vanilla (which contain alcohol)

- ◆ Laundry and dishwasher detergents

- ◆ Lighter fluid

- ◆ Oven cleaner

- ◆ Paint and turpentine

- ◆ Pesticides

- ◆ Pet medicine, vitamins and flea powder

- ◆ Plant fertilizer

- ◆ Scouring powder and toilet bowl cleaner

- ◆ Shoe polish

- ◆ Typewriter correction fluid

- ◆ Vinegar

For free "Mr. Yuk" poison warning stickers to attach to toxic household products, send a self-addressed stamped envelope to
Pittsburgh Poison Control Center
3705 Fifth Avenue
Pittsburgh, PA 15213.

 THE EXPERT: American Association of Poison Control Centers.

Lead poisoning has been called a "silent" disease because it usually doesn't cause any recognizable symptoms until the poisoning has become acute.

How to prevent lead poisoning

Lead poisoning is a widespread yet preventable disease affecting millions of preschoolers. Infants and young children are particularly vulnerable because their brains and nervous systems are still developing. Low levels of exposure can cause serious health and developmental consequences including reduced IQ and attention span, learning disabilities, and behavioral problems. In rare instances, severe lead poisoning can cause coma, convulsions or death.

◆ Test tap water for lead. Use cold water for all drinking and cooking — let it run for one minute before using. (Lead leaches more quickly into hot water.) Ask your pediatrician about using bottled water in baby formula.

◆ Serve foods high in iron (fortified cereal, leafy greens) and calcium (milk, cheese, broccoli) to combat the absorption of lead. Fatty fried foods let the body absorb lead more quickly.

◆ Do not store or serve food or beverages (especially acidic ones like orange juice) in imported pottery or ceramic dishes intended for decorative use; they may contain lead.

◆ Check painted toys and furniture for lead. Frequently wash objects infants put in their mouths in case they've come into contact with any lead dust.

The Centers for Disease Control and the American Academy of Pediatrics recommend that all children receive a lead test by 12 months and then every year through age 6.

Protect children from lead paint

A child can be poisoned by eating paint chips, as well as by dust from deteriorating or disturbed lead paint that gets on their hands and then into their mouths.

◆ Have your house tested for lead-based paint if it was built before 1978.

◆ Windows and other surfaces that abrade against each other can generate lead-contaminated dust. Wipe sills and the floor beneath weekly with a trisodium phosphate cleanser (available at hardware stores) or with a solution made from an automatic-dishwasher detergent that contains phosphate, like Sunlight, Cascade or Spic and Span (one tablespoon to one gallon of water).

◆ Test for the presence of lead paint before doing any renovation. If any is detected, use a certified contractor who is knowledgeable in lead-based paint removal. Remove or cover all household items while the work is in progress. Children and pregnant women should vacate the premises until work is completed and tests indicate it is safe.

Lead-based paint is the leading source of childhood lead poisoning. Although it was banned in 1978, it is still found in three out of four homes built before then.

• National Lead Information Center: 800-LEADFYI
• National Lead Clearinghouse: 800-424-LEAD
• EPA's Safe Drinking Water Hotline: 800-426-4791 (for the name of a local water-testing lab)

THE EXPERT: Alliance to End Childhood Lead Poisoning.

Under age 3, avoid toys or parts smaller than your child's fist. Toys must be larger than 1 1/4 inches in diameter; balls should be no smaller than 1 3/4 inches in diameter.

For a good quick safety test, use a toilet paper roll — if a toy fits through the hole it's too small for children under age 3.

Toy safety
What to avoid

◆ Lead paint or toxic materials

◆ Sharp points or edges

◆ Projectiles

◆ Strings longer than 12 inches

◆ Springs, gears or hinged parts that could pinch or entrap fingers

◆ Small parts that could detach, break or compress to fit into a child's mouth, nose or ears

◆ Exposed wires and parts that heat up

◆ Toys that make loud noises

What to (look) for . . .

◆ Manufacturers' recommended age
   guidelines advise you the toy may be
   unsafe for young children.

◆ The words "machine/surface washable"
   on stuffed and cloth toys, and "UL (Underwriters
   Laboratories) Approved" on electrical toys.

◆ Watch out for little toys and small parts that
   belong to an older child when there are
   younger siblings around.

◆ Examine toys regularly for damage — loose,
   chipped or cracked parts; sharp edges;
   splinters; loose seams — that may pose
   a hazard.

The Consumer Product
Safety Commission has
recorded information on
toys that have been
recalled or have a history
of safety problems. For
information or to report
an unsafe toy call
800-638-CPSC.

THE EXPERT: U. S. Consumer Product Safety Commission and Toy
Manufacturers of America, Inc.

LEARNING

It's never too early to begin reading to baby or to give baby books to explore on her own.

Choosing baby's first books

What to **look** for . . .

◆ Durability. Baby's first books will end up being chewed on, tossed around, and turned inside out, so choose sturdy cardboard, vinyl, or cloth books that won't be destroyed and can be wiped clean.

◆ Simple, clear, uncluttered illustrations and photographs of other babies, animals or familiar objects.

◆ Black-and-white or bright primary colors to help infants focus.

◆ Sensory appeal, so baby can touch or listen as you read. (Avoid all but the sturdiest pop-up or flap books until baby is old enough not to tear them apart. A better bet: a book that plays a tune to the touch.)

◆ Rhythm, repetition and rhyme. Babies love to hear the pattern of your voice, so look for books with narrative in addition to those that simply label objects.

Classic books every baby should know

- *Black on White* and *White on Black*
  by Tana Hoban (Greenwillow)

- *Max's First Word* (and other Max board books)
  by Rosemary Wells (Dial Books)

- *Chicka Chicka Boom Boom*
  by Bill Martin Jr. and John Archambault
  (Simon & Schuster)

- *Corduroy*
  by Don Freeman (Viking Penguin)

- *Pat the Bunny*
  by Dorothy Kunhardt (Golden Books)

- *Goodnight Moon*
  by Margaret Wise Brown (HarperCollins)

Make books come alive: be theatrical; imitate animal noises and everyday sounds; point out colors, shapes and objects; connect the illustrations to your baby's world by saying, "Here's the dog's nose; here's your nose."

THE EXPERT: Barbara Elleman, editor of *Book Links,* an American Library Association magazine.

Chapter Four

TODDLER
ONE–THREE YEARS

DAILY CARE

Bare feet are best to help your child's muscles develop. But once he's ready to walk outdoors it's time for the first pair of shoes or sneakers.

How to select your child's shoes

▶ Buy shoes late in the day because feet swell. Measure both feet for length and width; fit shoes for the larger foot.

▶ Don't buy by size alone. Each manufacturer has its own sizing. See how each pair looks, feels and fits.

▶ Make sure the heel of the shoe hugs the foot.

▶ Look for shoes with squared-off fronts that don't cramp toes. Shoes should be flexible to allow free foot movement.

▶ Don't buy oversized shoes your child will grow into — they can cause clumsiness and increase the risk of falls.

▶ Buy shoes made from natural, breathable materials like canvas and leather, which are cooler than synthetics.

▶ Use hand-me-down footwear only if it's almost new and hasn't molded to another child's foot.

To check for fit:
• While your child stands, pinch the shoe front — there should be room for your thumbnail (about 3/4 of an inch) between the longest toe and the end of the shoe.
• Press against the pinkie-toe side of each shoe — if you feel a bulge, the shoe is too narrow.

Time for new shoes

▶ Children's feet grow fast. Check shoes for proper fit every month until age 3; every four to six months from age 3 to 6 (more often if there's a growth spurt), and twice a year thereafter.

▶ Replace shoes when they become difficult to put on or the largest toe touches the tip. (As children grow, they tend to *wear* out rather than *grow* out of shoes.)

▶ When removing shoes, examine feet for redness, irritation or blisters indicating a shoe is too tight or may have a loose lining or irregular stitching.

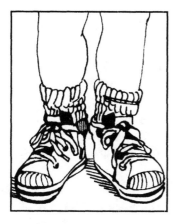

Teaching the difference between left and right

Marilise Flusser, author of *Party Shoes to School and Baseball Caps to Bed* (Fireside, 1992), offers these tips:

• Play the "happy feet" game: Show your child how a pair of shoes placed together incorrectly arch away from each other. When put together correctly they're so happy the toes "kiss!"

• Make or buy "Left" and "Right" shoe stickers for inside your child's shoes.

• Draw a puzzle picture that starts on the left sneaker (a dinosaur's head) and continues on the right (the body and tail). The picture is complete when the sneakers are put together correctly.

• Draw a design with permanent ink on the instep of each sneaker. Your child will know they're on the correct feet when the designs touch.

THE EXPERT: American Podiatric Medical Association.

There is no right age to begin toilet training. Let a child's behavior and psychological readiness determine when he's ready, not solely his age or the fact that all his friends are doing it.

Toilet training

▶ Take your child shopping for a potty. Explain what it's used for and that it's his own. Keep it easily accessible.

▶ Together, read books and watch videos about going to the potty.

▶ Let your child get familiar with the potty: let him sit on it while dressed and then undressed.

▶ Suggest that your child sit on the potty at regular daily times: upon awakening, after breakfast, midmorning, after lunch, midafternoon, after supper, and before bed.

▶ Let him sit there for several minutes. Don't force him to stay if nothing happens.

▶ If he resists using the potty after several weeks he may not be ready. Try again in a few weeks.

▶ Once toilet training begins, switch to disposable or washable training pants.

▶ Praise successful efforts. Some parents use rewards; others believe a parent's pride and approval, combined with the child's feeling of independence, are reward enough.

▶ Expect accidents. Never punish, criticize or ridicule a slow learner. Change your child quickly and say, "You'll get better at this."

▶ Celebrate after a few successful weeks; let him/her select some "big boy/girl" underwear.

Signs of readiness

Children exhibit signs that they're ready to be toilet trained between 18 months and 3 years. You'll know when your child:

▶ Has regular and predictable bowel movements.

▶ Stays dry for at least two hours at a time.

▶ Wakes up dry after naps.

▶ Complains about wet or dirty diapers.

▶ Lets you know through facial expression, posture or words when he has to urinate or have a bowel movement.

▶ Is curious about the toilet and understands its purpose.

▶ Wants to imitate parents, friends or siblings.

▶ Asks to use the toilet or potty.

▶ Requests "big boy/girl" underwear.

Training tips

• Delay training during major family changes like a move or a new sibling.

• Summer is a good time to train, when children can play naked or lightly clothed for quick potty visits.

• Dress your child in easy-on, easy-off clothes.

• Work with your caregiver or day care center for a consistent training routine. Make sure you use the same words to describe body parts and functions.

• Help boys learn to aim by floating a square of toilet paper in the toilet bowl.

• If your son is afraid of the toilet, reassure him that only his urine and bowel movement will be flushed away and nothing will happen to his body. (Boys are usually more anxious about this.)

THE EXPERT: Joae Graham Brooks, M.D., assistant clinical professor of psychiatry at Harvard Medical School and author of *No More Diapers!* (Bantam Doubleday Dell, 1991).

Stain removal tips

Blood	Soak in cold water for 30 minutes. Pretreat any remaining stain and launder in hottest water safe for fabric. If stain remains, soak in warm water with a presoaking product.
Chewing gum	Rub with ice. Remove excess with a dull knife and sponge with cleaning fluid. Rinse and launder in hottest water possible.
Chocolate	Soak in cold water. Pretreat remaining stain. Launder using hottest water possible and appropriate bleach. If stain remains, sponge with a cleaning fluid; rinse and launder again.
Crayon	Place stained area facedown on a bunch of paper towels. Spray with WD-40 and let stand for a few minutes. Turn fabric over and spray the other side; let stand. Work liquid hand soap into the stain until removed. Hand wash to remove WD-40. Rinse and launder.

Grass	Pretreat stain. Launder in hottest water safe for fabric. If stain remains, sponge with rubbing alcohol. (If colorfastness is questionable or fabric is acetate, dilute alcohol with two parts water.) Rinse and launder.
Ink	Sponge stain with rubbing alcohol or spray with a pretreating product or hair spray. Rinse thoroughly. Pretreat stain and launder in hottest water safe for fabric with appropriate bleach.
Milk and ice cream	Soak in warm water. Launder in hot water and use appropriate bleach. If grease stain remains, sponge with cleaning fluid. Rinse and launder.

Loosen gum stuck in hair with a glob of
creamy peanut butter or a few
dabs of mineral or vegetable oil, says Carol
Kushner, owner of Shortcuts, a
children's hair salon in New York City.
Then gently comb it out.

THE EXPERT: Maytag Consumer Education.

111

FEEDING

How to feed a picky eater

▶ Hide the vegetables: puree or grate them into soups, sauces, muffins and breads.

▶ Make good-for-you foods fun and appealing: serve a scoop of cottage cheese topped with fruit in an ice cream cone; make a funny face with pea eyes, carrot nose and bean sprout hair; have a yogurt sundae-making party, or make fruit kabobs.

▶ Let kids help: they'll eat what they helped make or grow.

▶ Don't overwhelm: serve small portions on a large plate so it doesn't look like too much; your child can always ask for seconds.

▶ Serve child-friendly miniatures: mini hamburgers, cocktail bread finger sandwiches, baby corn and tiny new potatoes.

Do . . .

▶ Offer praise for trying new foods. Introduce new foods alongside old favorites.

▶ Provide role models: let your child see you and his peers experimenting with different foods.

▶ Serve foods in different ways: instead of cooked carrots try raw carrot sticks with a yogurt dip, shred carrots in a salad, or make carrot juice.

▶ Let your child stop eating when he's full even if his plate isn't clean.

Don't . . .

▶ Give up if your child doesn't like a food once; offer it again and again. After repeated exposure he may try it.

▶ Force your child to eat anything he doesn't want.

▶ Plead, beg or reward the eating of certain foods.

▶ Tell him to "Please eat another bite," or "You can't leave the table till you finish." This teaches your child to ignore internal cues about when to stop eating, which can lead to overeating and obesity.

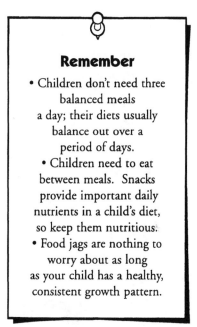

Remember

• Children don't need three balanced meals a day; their diets usually balance out over a period of days.
• Children need to eat between meals. Snacks provide important daily nutrients in a child's diet, so keep them nutritious.
• Food jags are nothing to worry about as long as your child has a healthy, consistent growth pattern.

THE EXPERT: Children's Nutrition Research Center, Baylor College of Medicine, Houston.

The more you make an issue out of a food that your child doesn't like, the more you make sure he'll never eat it again. Relax. There's no one food your child must have in order to survive.

Food substitutions

Consider substitution as your best strategy to make sure your child gets all the nutrients he needs.

If your child won't drink milk

Make sure he gets calcium in other ways:

- ▶ Cheese

- ▶ Yogurt

- ▶ Frozen yogurt or light ice cream

- ▶ Calcium-fortified juices

- ▶ Cream-based soups

- ▶ Dark green, leafy vegetables like broccoli, spinach, kale and romaine lettuce

- ▶ Tofu

- ▶ Ricotta

For answers to your food and nutrition questions or for a referral to a registered dietitian in your area, call the American Dietetic Association nutrition hotline: 800-366-1655.

If your child won't eat meat

As a protein substitute try:

- Eggs
- Chicken
- Fish
- Cheese
- Cottage cheese

- Peanut butter
- Cooked dried peas and beans
- Tofu
- Nuts (for children over age 4)

How to make sure your child gets enough iron

Good iron sources beyond vitamins:

- Red meats and liver
- Enriched whole-grain breads and cereals
- Dried fruit
- Wheat germ

- Dark green, leafy vegetables, including spinach, chard and kale
- Cooked dried peas and beans

 THE EXPERT: Jo-Ann Heslin, registered dietitian and nutrition consultant; coauthor of *No-Nonsense Nutrition for Kids* (Pocket Books, 1985).

Nutritious Alternatives

If your child won't eat . . .	Try instead . . .	Nutritional value
Spinach Broccoli Tomato Red pepper	Watermelon Papaya Cantaloupe Persimmon	Excellent sources of vitamins A and C
Sweet potato Carrots Winter squash Pumpkin	Apricot Mango Peach Nectarine	Excellent sources of vitamin A
Green pepper Brussels sprouts Cabbage Cauliflower Potato	Orange Tangerine Grapefruit Guava Strawberries	Excellent sources of vitamin C
Green beans Peas Lima beans Turnips	Banana Apple Pear Grapes	Good sources of potassium and fair sources of A, C and the B vitamin group

 THE EXPERT: Jo-Ann Heslin, registered dietitian and nutrition consultant; coauthor of *No-Nonsense Nutrition for Kids* (Pocket Books, 1985).

The worst snacks for teeth

The worst snacks for your child's teeth are high in starch and sugar (worse than sugar alone), which allow bacteria in the mouth to form tooth-destroying acids. Sticky foods, too, do a lot of damage because they stay on teeth a long time.

Take special care after eating:

- Gooey candy (like toffee)
- Raisins and dried fruit
- Granola bars
- Peanut butter
- Salted crackers
- Caramel popcorn
- Oatmeal and cream-sandwich cookies

Safe snacks for teeth:

- Cheddar, Swiss and other hard cheeses
- Apples, carrots, celery
- Grapes and plums (instead of raisins and prunes)
- Nuts (for children over age 4)

Keeping your child's teeth cavity free takes more than instituting a candy ban. In fact, some candies do a lot less damage to teeth than seemingly good-for-you foods like crackers and raisins.

The best way to keep teeth clean is to brush right after eating. If your child can't brush, water or milk will help wash away some residue. Also helpful is eating a piece of cheese, an apple or other fruit to lift off bits of ground-in food. Chewing sugarless gum after a meal or snack stimulates saliva, which washes away food particles and neutralizes bacterial acids.

THE EXPERT: American Society of Dentistry for Children.

Cholesterol is not only an adult problem. Although it poses no immediate health problems for most children, those with high levels may be at greater risk for strokes, heart disease and other circulatory problems when they grow up.

Kids and cholesterol

▶ The American Academy of Pediatrics recommends testing blood cholesterol levels of only those children whose parents have a high cholesterol level (over 240) or who come from a family with a history of heart disease before age 55.

▶ These children should be tested after age 2; before that they need a high-fat diet for proper development.

▶ If your child has an elevated level, do a second test to be sure. If that is also high you will likely be advised to monitor your child's body weight and cholesterol level, and make sure he regularly exercises and follows a standard low-fat, low-cholesterol diet.

▶ Children not in the high-risk category can have their cholesterol tested around age 10.

▶ All healthy children should follow a regular routine of physical activity and (over age 2) follow a balanced low-fat, low-cholesterol diet with approximately 30 percent of their total calories from fat (with fewer than 10 percent of those from saturated fat, found in beef, butter, cheese, hydrogenated shortening, and coconut and palm oils).

How to have a low-fat, low-cholesterol diet

▶ Serve 99 percent fat-free (1% low-fat milk) or skim milk to children over age 2.

▶ Substitute part-skim mozzarella for higher fat cheeses like American or Swiss.

▶ Offer frozen yogurt instead of ice cream.

▶ Serve lots of raw or steamed vegetables.

▶ Eat whole grains.

▶ Use chopped chicken or turkey instead of beef.

▶ Choose low-fat sandwich meats and lean cuts of beef or pork.

▶ Serve fish and skinless poultry frequently.

▶ The American Heart Association says that children can eat up to four egg yolks a week plus unlimited whites. (To make scrambled eggs with lower cholesterol, use one whole egg and one white.)

▶ Have a minimum of fast food.

▶ Provide low-fat snacks like fig cookies, graham crackers, rice cakes, pretzels, popcorn and whole-grain cereals.

 THE EXPERT: Dr. Myron Winick, Williams Professor of Nutrition (emeritus), Columbia University College of Physicians and Surgeons, and author of *Growing Up Healthy: A Parent's Guide to Good Nutrition* (William Morrow and Co., 1982).

HEALTH

Call 911 or your emergency number for any severely injured child.

Quick first aid tips

Animal or human bites

▶ Wash wound thoroughly with soap and water.

▶ If skin is punctured or lacerated, call your doctor. (If your child is bitten by a pet, get the name, address and phone number of the animal's owner. If bitten by a wild animal, contain it if possible without endangering yourself, so health officials can examine it.)

Burns

▶ Apply cool, running water or clean, cool, wet towels (change them constantly to keep area wet and cool).

▶ Do not use ice, butter or grease.

▶ Apply a dry, sterile dressing.

▶ Call doctor if blisters appear (do not break), or for any burn on the face, hands, feet or genitals.

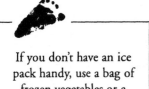

If you don't have an ice pack handy, use a bag of frozen vegetables or a Popsicle, or keep a few miniature packs of soy sauce or mustard from a fast food restaurant in your freezer for a quick fix for a small bump or bruise.

Choking (over age 1)

If your child is choking, but can still breathe, speak or cough, call your doctor for further advice before doing anything.

First aid for choking is necessary only if the child's airway is blocked so completely that he cannot cry, cough, breathe or speak, or is coughing weakly or making high-pitched sounds. In that case, start rescue efforts and then call 911 or your emergency number.

▶ Stand behind the child to do the Heimlich maneuver.

▶ Wrap your arms around the child's waist.

▶ Place the thumb side of your fist against the middle of the abdomen just above the navel and below the rib cage.

▶ Grasp fist with other hand and give five quick upward thrusts. Repeat until child can breathe or he coughs up the object.

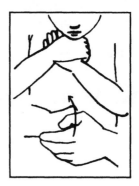

THE EXPERT: American Red Cross.

Cuts and scrapes

▶ Apply pressure to the wound with a clean cloth.

▶ If the cut is large and deep, call your local emergency number.

▶ For minor cuts, wash with soap and water. Apply a bandage.

▶ Call the doctor if bleeding continues.

▶ Watch for signs of infection — pus, fever, swelling or tenderness.

Nosebleeds

▶ Have the child sit erect, leaning forward.

▶ Squeeze the nostrils together between your thumb and index finger until bleeding stops.

▶ If bleeding doesn't stop, call your doctor.

Bone and muscle injuries

▶ Keep the injured part from moving.

▶ To reduce pain and prevent swelling, apply a cold pack to the injury site and seek medical care.

Use a red or dark-colored washcloth to clean a bloody cut so your child won't be frightened by seeing a bloodied cloth.

Poisoning

▶ Call emergency number or Poison Control Center immediately.

▶ Explain what substance the child may have swallowed; if available, give brand and manufacturer name.

▶ Supply child's age and weight.

▶ Follow instructions before inducing vomiting or administering syrup of ipecac.

Head injuries

▶ If child is not alert, doesn't respond, or continues to cry for a long period, get immediate medical attention. Keep him as still as possible if you suspect a head, neck or back injury and call 911 or your emergency number.

▶ If a head injury is minor, apply ice to the injured area and continue to watch the child closely during the next 24 hours. Call your doctor if there is persistent sleepiness, lethargy, dilating pupils, vomiting, oozing blood or clear fluid from ears or nose, convulsions, or loss of consciousness.

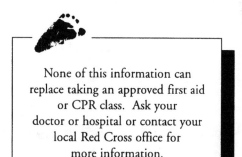

None of this information can replace taking an approved first aid or CPR class. Ask your doctor or hospital or contact your local Red Cross office for more information.

THE EXPERT: American Red Cross.

How to have a stress-free doctor's visit

▶ Make the first appointment in the morning or right after the doctor's lunch break and you'll have a shorter wait. Also, ask which is the slowest day of the week (it's usually Tuesdays, Wednesdays or Thursdays).

▶ Stay upbeat and calm so your child doesn't sense any anxiety you may have.

▶ Help your child anticipate doctor visits by saying, "Let's find out how much you've grown."

▶ Playact with a toy doctor's kit.

Suggestions

• **Don't say:** "You're going to get a shot."
• **Do say:** "You're going to get an injection."

• **Don't say:** "It won't hurt."
• **Do say:** "It will be quick."

• **Don't say:** "The more you move, the longer this will take."
• **Do say:** "Your job is to hold still so this will be over with quickly."

• **Don't say:** "If you don't behave, you won't get a treat."
• **Do say:** "As soon as the exam is over, we can get ice cream."

▶ Don't lie — "It won't hurt" — or make promises you can't keep — "You won't get an injection today" — or you'll lose your child's trust.

▶ Dress your child in easy-off clothing.

▶ Give your child some control by offering choices when possible — "Which ear should the doctor look in first?"

▶ Use positive reinforcement: "You're being very brave." "It's almost over."

▶ Praise your child for his cooperation.

▶ If your child has an extremely bad reaction to his pediatrician, or you're not happy with the doctor's bedside manner, consider switching doctors.

Chicken pox, a highly contagious disease that was once a rite of childhood, may soon be only a memory thanks to a vaccine recently approved by the Food and Drug Administration. The American Academy of Pediatrics recommends that children receive it between the ages of 12 and 18 months. A booster shot may later be necessary. Ask your doctor for more information.

 THE EXPERT: Dr. Philip C. Kendall, director of the Child and Adolescent Anxiety Clinic at Temple University, Philadelphia.

Although many trips to the hospital are for unexpected emergencies, if your child needs a planned visit, prepare him so he knows what to expect. Children are frightened by the unknown.

Help the staff communicate with your child: Provide a list with his nickname, favorite activities, habits, fears, plus the words and phrases he uses for his pacifier, the bathroom, pain, etc.

Preparing your child for hospitalization

Before you go

▶ Prepare a young child only a week or so in advance so he has less time to worry.

▶ Explain why your child is going to the hospital and what will happen, in simple, age-appropriate terms.

▶ Encourage questions.

▶ Tell the truth and use accurate but not too detailed explanations. If there will be pain, say so, but explain that it will soon go away.

▶ Reassure your child that he's not being punished for his illness.

▶ Take a hospital tour and meet the staff.

▶ Read books or watch videos together on the subject.

▶ Play "hospital" with dolls and a toy doctor's kit to help your child express his feelings and concerns.

When you go

▶ Let your child pack a few special things like toys, books, pillow and family photos.

▶ Don't forget his security blanket, night-light, favorite juice cup, and other comfort items.

▶ Pack healthy snacks so family members don't have to rely on vending machine munchies.

▶ Bring a tape recorder and familiar tapes, plus taped messages from family and friends.

▶ Contact the hospital's support system (counselors, therapists, etc.) to help you and your child cope.

▶ Tell your child whether you will be staying with him at the hospital. When you can't be there, let him know where you'll be and when you'll be back.

▶ Explain that as soon as your child feels better he will be coming home.

When you return home

▶ Plan a welcome home celebration.

▶ Talk about what happened in the hospital and encourage your child to continue playing "hospital" to act out any lingering fears or concerns.

The Association for the Care of Children's Health offers dozens of brochures on the social, emotional and psychological needs of children in health care settings. Call 800-808-2224.

 THE EXPERT: Association for the Care of Children's Health.

Lyme disease is a bacterial infection caused by the bite of an infected tick.

Lyme disease

Diagnosis of Lyme disease is difficult because tests are not reliable and no single symptom appears in all cases, nor within any predictable time span. Plus, people often don't even realize they were bitten.

The clearest sign of infection (which occurs in about 50 percent of all cases) is a red, bull's-eye-shaped rash that can develop from three to 32 days after the infection has been contracted. Other early indicators — including flulike fever, chills and achiness — mimic other diseases.

If caught early, Lyme disease can often be treated with antibiotics. Left untreated, it can cause serious health problems, including severe fatigue, chronic headaches, joint disease and neurological problems.

Prevention

▶ Dress children in hats, long-sleeved shirts and long pants (tucked into socks) when playing in the woods or tall grassy areas.

▶ Stay on trails when hiking. Avoid tall grass and brush.

▶ Apply tick repellent to clothing and exposed skin, avoiding face and hands. (The American Academy of Pediatrics recommends that children use products containing 10 percent or less of the ingredient DEET.) Wash off at day's end.

▶ Do a body check after children play outside, especially in high-risk areas during tick season. Ticks can be as small as poppy seeds and may look like freckles or specks of dirt. Look behind ears and knees, under arms, on scalp, and around the groin.

▶ If you remove a tick promptly your chances of getting Lyme disease are greatly reduced. To remove a tick, grasp it close to the skin with a fine-tipped tweezers; pull straight out. Disinfect the area with alcohol or an antibiotic ointment. Save the tick for testing.

▶ If you suspect your child has been bitten by a tick, see a doctor immediately.

Tick season is usually May through August, though it varies in different parts of the country.

THE EXPERT: Lyme Disease Foundation, Inc.

Poison ivy, poison sumac and poison oak

You can develop a rash from these plants without even coming into contact with them. Urushiol, the colorless oil that oozes from the plants and their sap and causes the rash, is very easily spread. Sticky and virtually invisible, it can be carried on the fur of animals, on garden tools, and on sports equipment that have come into contact with a crushed or broken plant. It can even spread in the wind if a plant is burned in a fire.

Once it touches the skin, urushiol begins to penetrate in minutes. A rash will appear within 12 to 48 hours and takes about 10 days to heal.

Teach children to recognize and avoid poison ivy, poison sumac and poison oak. Although the saying "Leaves of three, let them be" is a good rule of thumb, the plants take on different appearances depending on the environment and season; leaves may also come in groups of five, seven or nine. Get to know what they look like in your area.

Treatment

▶ Immediately wash exposed areas with soap and cold water. If you do so within five to 10 minutes of exposure you can keep the urushiol from spreading.

▶ Wash all tools or equipment that may have come in contact with urushiol; it remains active for months.

▶ To soothe a rash, take cool showers, soak in a lukewarm bath with an oatmeal or baking soda solution, and use calamine lotion.

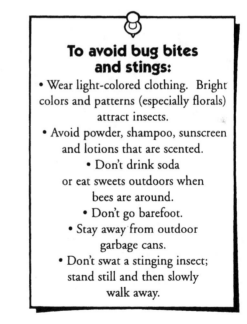

To avoid bug bites and stings:

• Wear light-colored clothing. Bright colors and patterns (especially florals) attract insects.
• Avoid powder, shampoo, sunscreen and lotions that are scented.
• Don't drink soda or eat sweets outdoors when bees are around.
• Don't go barefoot.
• Stay away from outdoor garbage cans.
• Don't swat a stinging insect; stand still and then slowly walk away.

THE EXPERT: American Academy of Dermatology.

Sun care

Repeated exposure to the sun, even in a child's early years, has a lifelong effect and can ultimately lead to premature aging of the skin, skin cancer and other problems.

For the first year, keep baby out of the sun as much as possible. With older children:

▶ Try to limit exposure to the sun from 10 A.M. to 3 P.M., when the sun's rays are strongest.

▶ Cover up with wide-brimmed hats and clothing.

▶ Choose a sunscreen with an SPF of 15 or greater in a milky lotion or cream. Clear lotions may contain alcohol, which can sting. (Sunscreen is not recommended for infants under 6 months.)

▶ Before using a sunscreen, test it by placing a small amount on the underside of your child's forearm or abdomen. If there's any irritation, try a different brand. (Some children react to ingredients like PABA, lanolin or perfume.)

▶ Half an hour before your child goes outdoors apply a liberal amount of sunscreen to his entire body, or put it on your naked child before he gets dressed.

▶ Don't forget ears, scalp, instep, and the back of the neck and knees. Use a sunscreen lip balm for lips.

▶ Don't apply sunscreen on or near eyelids.

▶ Make sure sunscreen doesn't get on a child's fingers and end up in his mouth or eyes.

▶ Reapply sunscreen as per directions. Choose a waterproof sunscreen when your child goes swimming.

▶ Although skin cancer is extremely rare in young children, examine your child's skin regularly for any new raised growths, itchy patches, nonhealing sores or changes in moles. If you notice any, show the doctor.

▶ Be a role model; practice sensible sun care habits yourself.

☞ THE EXPERT: The Skin Cancer Foundation.

Ears

Spotting a hearing problem

Have a toddler between 12 months and 2 years evaluated by a specialist if he:

▶ Does not respond to sound, turn in the direction of a soft voice, or seem able to locate where sound is coming from.

▶ Does not begin to imitate and use simple words for familiar people and things.

▶ Does not use speech or sound like other children his age.

▶ Does not show consistent growth in the understanding and use of words to communicate.

Ears and flying

If your toddler experiences discomfort during pressure changes when flying:

▶ Wake him when the plane is descending. Children swallow less often when asleep.

▶ Tell him to yawn or swallow often.

▶ Let him drink, chew gum or suck a candy.

▶ Try unblocking your child's ears by pinching his nose shut while he blows air gently through the nostrils.

Ear care guidelines

▶ **Ear infections:** Very common in young children. Symptoms: pain (children may tug at their ears), high fever and extreme irritability. Left untreated, ear infections can result in punctured eardrums or even hearing loss. For chronic infections your doctor may suggest the surgical placement of tiny plastic tubes in the eardrum to help drain the fluid.

▶ **Ear wax:** Never insert a cotton swab or other instrument into the ear canal. Wax comes to the surface; simply clean the outside ear folds.

▶ **Foreign bodies:** Do not try to remove an object from your child's ear unless it is easily grasped because you may push it deeper. See your doctor.

▶ **Insects:** If an insect flies into an ear, apply a drop of mineral oil to immobilize it. It should float out.

▶ **Swimmer's ear:** To prevent this painful condition, have children tilt their heads from side to side to shake out excess water after swimming. A few drops of rubbing alcohol in the ear canal helps water evaporate.

▶ **Noise:** Don't let children hold noise-producing toys near their ears. Monitor the volume of radios and tape players — if you can hear the music while your child is wearing a headset, it's too loud.

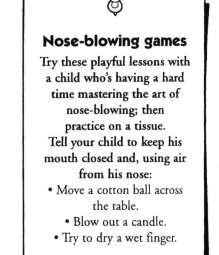

Nose-blowing games

Try these playful lessons with a child who's having a hard time mastering the art of nose-blowing; then practice on a tissue.
Tell your child to keep his mouth closed and, using air from his nose:
• Move a cotton ball across the table.
• Blow out a candle.
• Try to dry a wet finger.

THE EXPERT: American Academy of Otolaryngology — Head and Neck Surgery, Inc.

SAFETY

Choking prevention

▶ Do not feed children under 4 years any round, firm foods unless they're cut into small pieces.

▶ Insist that children eat while sitting at the table and never walk, run or play with food in their mouths.

▶ Teach young children to chew thoroughly before swallowing.

▶ Supervise mealtime.

▶ Learn the Heimlich maneuver to use on a choking child over age 1.

▶ Be vigilant about picking up and safely storing an older sibling's small toys and parts when there's a younger child around.

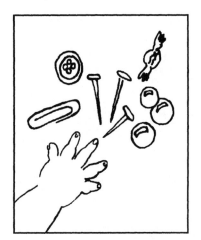

Choking hazards

## Food	## Objects
▶ Raw carrots	▶ Balloons
▶ Hot dogs	▶ Coins
▶ Chunks of meat	▶ Marbles
▶ Popcorn	▶ Small toys and parts
▶ Hard candies	▶ Pen caps
▶ Nuts	▶ Small batteries
▶ Raisins	▶ Pins and paper clips
▶ Whole grapes	▶ Buttons
▶ Spoonfuls of peanut butter	▶ Nails and screws

Before serving hot dogs, always cut lengthwise and then crosswise into small pieces. Removing the casing also helps children chew and swallow hot dogs better.

THE EXPERT: *American Academy of Pediatrics.*

Christmas safety

▶ Keep tree ornaments high up where children can't reach them. Avoid fragile glass ornaments and strings of cranberries and popcorn, which children can choke on.

▶ Use only UL-approved lights and no more than three strings of lights per extension cord.

▶ Check for frayed wires, cracked sockets and loose connections.

▶ Unplug lights when you go to bed or leave the house.

▶ Use tinsel or artificial icicles made of unleaded, nonflammable material. Angel hair can irritate eyes and skin and artificial snow can irritate lungs.

▶ Make sure a live tree is fresh: look for sap on the trunk, needles that don't break, and not too many dry, falling needles. Keep tree moist. Secure to wall or ceiling for extra stability.

▶ Make sure an artificial tree is labeled "fire resistant."

▶ When opening gifts, immediately dispose of ribbons, plastic bags, wrapping paper, staples and pins.

THE EXPERT: National Safety Council.

Water safety

▶ Never leave children unsupervised or out of eye contact in or near any body of water.

▶ Learn CPR.

▶ Don't consider children "drownproof" because they know how to swim or are wearing flotation devices.

▶ Completely enclose your pool or spa with a fence with a self-closing, self-latching gate. Latches should be out of children's reach. (Check state and local safety regulations.)

▶ Install a safety cover and make sure it is always closed when your pool or spa is not in use and completely removed when in use.

▶ Drain standing water from a pool cover. Empty and turn wading pools upside down when not in use.

▶ Remove all floating toys from pool when not in use. An unsupervised child may try to retrieve them.

▶ Keep a phone and rescue equipment nearby.

THE EXPERT: National Spa and Pool Institute.

Set a safe example — let your child see that you always fasten your safety belt.

How to keep your child seated

It can be tough to get squirmy toddlers into their car seats and keep them there happily. Make the practice mandatory and routine whether you're riding down the street or on the highway, so your child learns that the car doesn't move until everyone is buckled in.

▶ Make sure the car seat is comfortable. Adjust straps as your child grows and when he's wearing bulky winter clothes, so they are snug but not tight.

▶ Protect your child from metal buckles that get hot in the sun — keep them covered. If the sun bothers sensitive eyes, attach a window shade.

▶ Provide diversion with soft toys and books that can't hurt your child in case of a sudden stop. (Attach to the car seat with plastic links.)

▶ As soon as your child is buckled in, make it a routine to turn on a favorite tape.

▶ Let your child buckle a doll or stuffed animal into the seat next to him.

▶ Make your child a Safety Belt Deputy who checks that everyone is safely buckled — this will give him some control over the situation.

From 1 to 4 years and up to 40 pounds, children should sit in a forward-facing car seat. When you turn around a convertible seat, move it into the upright position; adjust shoulder straps to a higher slot (usually the top set), and put the safety belt in the proper path.

THE EXPERT: SafetyBeltSafe U.S.A.

How safe is your playground?

▶ It is kept free of debris.

▶ Equipment is well maintained and regularly checked for loose or missing parts, rust, corrosion or deterioration.

▶ There is protective surfacing under and around all equipment — rubber matting, wood chips, sand or gravel.

▶ Equipment is not too close together or to other objects and is stable and anchored securely.

▶ Elevated platforms have guardrails if over 20 inches high for preschoolers, or 30 inches high for school-age children.

▶ Swings are made of lightweight plastic or rubber.

▶ Equipment has no sharp points, corners, edges, protrusions or exposed moving parts.

▶ Spaces or bars in equipment are less than 3 1/2 inches or more than nine inches apart.

Installation, maintenance, layout and design of equipment are all important elements in a playground. If you think your local playground doesn't meet safety standards and presents a hazard to children, alert school or park officials.

Backyard safety

To cushion falls, install backyard play equipment on a protective covering of nine inches of wood chips, pea gravel or sand that extends six feet from the perimeter in all directions. Grass is too hard. Rake sandy surfaces after it rains and replace material yearly.

 THE EXPERT: John Preston, mechanical engineer and coauthor of the *Handbook for Public Playground Safety* for the U.S. Consumer Product Safety Commission.

COPING

Moving from crib to bed

Between the ages of 2 and 3, your toddler may be ready to move from a crib to a bed. You'll know it's time when he/she begins climbing out of the crib or asking for a "big boy/girl" bed. Don't initiate the switch in the middle of another big change like a move or a new baby. Make it easier by starting with naps in the bed.

To make the transition easier, some cribs have removable sides that convert it to a bed. You can also purchase a junior bed. If you're moving to a standard-size bed, make sure your child is physically able to get in and out of it on his own.

▶ Talk about the move in advance. Appeal to your child's pride in growing up: "What a big boy/girl you are to sleep in a bed."

▶ If possible, set up the bed before you take the crib down to help your child get used to the change. Children grow attached to their cribs.

▶ Have a good-bye ceremony for the crib.

▶ Go shopping together for new bedding but also keep familiar objects like stuffed animals or a favorite blanket.

▶ Use side rails or pile pillows on the floor next to the bed so your child doesn't worry about falling out.

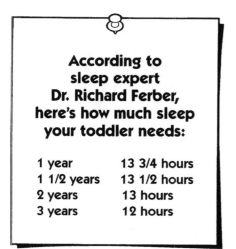

According to sleep expert Dr. Richard Ferber, here's how much sleep your toddler needs:

1 year	13 3/4 hours
1 1/2 years	13 1/2 hours
2 years	13 hours
3 years	12 hours

THE EXPERT: Nancy Balaban, Ed.D., director of the Infant and Parent Development Program at Bank Street Graduate School of Education, New York.

Getting children to help is easier when you are clear about what you want and realistic about your expectations.

How to get children to help around the house

▶ Assign tasks to fit the age, ability and experience of each child.

▶ Expect children to go through stages as they grow: children as young as 2 can help with a task; by age 5, they'll do it when reminded or supervised, and by age 10, they'll do it alone.

▶ Divide tasks into manageable pieces. If it's overwhelming, most children won't start. Instead of "Clean up your toys," say, "Put your trucks and cars in the toy box and your books on the shelves."

▶ Explain the task clearly: "When the timer rings, it will be time to put your dolls back in the toy box."

▶ Offer choices. Children are more willing to help if they've been involved in the decision: "Do you want to put away the trucks or the books first?"

▶ Set reasonable deadlines tied to an event, rather than a specific time: "Put your toys on the shelf so we can go to the park."

▶ Create a reminder system: set the timer, post a progress chart, or sing a transition song ("Time to put the toys away," to the tune of "Mary had a little lamb").

▶ Make tasks a routine part of the daily schedule.

▶ Establish consequences in advance: "What will I say if you ask to have a friend over and your room isn't clean?"

▶ Encourage cooperation. Use praise or set up an incentive system: put a marble in a jar for each job completed; when the jar is full your child gets to choose a treat.

Make helping fun

▶ Turn cleanup into a game: put away all the red toys; then all the blue ones.

▶ Turn on music and dance or sing as you work.

▶ Use mittens or hand puppets to help put things away.

▶ Hang a hoop over the hamper and play basketball with dirty clothes.

Chores your child can do

Age 2-3
• Help put toys away.
• Help tear lettuce for a salad.
• Put clothes in hamper.

Age 4-5
• Undress self.
• Pull up covers on own bed.
• Clear place setting from the table.
• Help use carrot scraper to clean vegetables.
• Help sort laundry into white and dark piles.

THE EXPERT: Elizabeth Crary, parent educator and author of *Pick Up Your Socks . . . and Other Skills Growing Children Need!* (Parenting Press, 1990).

Relocating can be stressful for young children who don't really understand what's happening, who fear the unknown, and who may have a hard time coping with change. To reduce any anxiety, you'll need to prepare them.

Ask the former residents of your new home to leave directions to nearby playgrounds and the names of local children and baby-sitters.

Making moving manageable

Before you go

▶ About a month before, explain where you are moving and reassure your child that he will be coming with you and so will his toys and possessions.

▶ Explain how everything will get from the old house to the new one.

▶ Take your child to see his new home — show him where he will sleep, eat and play — or show him photos.

▶ Make a videotape of your old house, neighborhood and friends.

▶ Exchange addresses. Tell your child that he can write, call and/or visit.

▶ Take out library books about moving and encourage your child to talk about his feelings.

▶ Let him decide which of his possessions, if any, he wants to discard. Familiar items will help him adjust.

▶ Let your child help: he can pack nonbreakables and label boxes with drawings of what's inside.

Moving day

▶ Give your child his own suitcase to pack the special possessions that will travel with him.

▶ Also pack a bag with toothbrushes, towels, pajamas, night-light, security objects, pillows, and sheets to keep with you during the move so children can settle in fast.

▶ Walk through the house to say a final good-bye. Acknowledge that you, too, are sad to leave.

When you arrive

▶ Make a ceremony of entering the new house.

▶ Set up your child's room first. Arrange furnishings as they were in his old room to give a sense of familiarity.

▶ Later, include your child in plans to redecorate.

▶ Stick to as many routines as possible.

▶ Expect changes in eating, sleeping, and toilet-training patterns before and after a move. Be patient; things will soon return to normal.

• Ryder Truck Rental sells a video for children, *Let's Get a Move On*.
Call: 800-615-3999.
• Mayflower Transit, Inc., offers *My Move*, a free game, story, and sticker kit. Call your local representative.
• The American Movers Conference publishes a free guide, *Moving and Children*. Send a SASE to 1611 Duke Street Alexandria, VA 22314.

THE EXPERT: Beverly Roman, family relocation expert and author of *Moving Minus Mishaps* (BR Anchor Publishing, 1992).

Early separations can be hard on parents as well as children, but you can smooth the way.

Easing separation anxiety

Gentle good-byes

▶ Make time in the morning to cuddle, play or talk before you leave.

▶ If your caregiver comes to your home, have her arrive at least 15 minutes early so she and your child can start an activity before you leave.

▶ Give your child something of yours to keep with him — a scarf, key chain, family photo, etc.

▶ Create a good-bye ritual — kiss a special spot, sing a song, or rub noses.

▶ Never sneak off. Say good-bye, adding, "I'll see you soon" or "See you later, alligator."

▶ Peg your return to a specific activity, not a time: "after lunch" or "when naptime is over."

▶ To ease away, tell your child you will leave in five minutes, "when the big hand on the clock is on the three."

▶ Don't prolong your parting; say good-bye and go, even if your child protests.

Most of these suggestions are for parents who work outside the home and leave children with a caregiver or at a day care center, but they work for occasional separations as well.

Happy hellos

After a long day at work, you're exhausted, but you're looking forward to seeing your child. Then when you pick him up at day care, school, or from a caregiver he ignores you, rejects your requests to get ready, or starts wailing. Children act out most with the people they trust, so realize this is a normal part of child development.

How to survive the evening homecoming:

▶ On your trip home from work, listen to music, read a magazine, or do something that helps you switch gears.

▶ Start a homecoming ritual: read a story, take a walk, or dance away the day's tensions with your child.

▶ If you have to do chores or start dinner the minute you return home, get your children involved.

Don't rush your child away at day's end from day care, school or play dates. To help him make a smooth transition, let him complete his activity, show you his artwork, and say good-bye to his caregiver, teacher or friends. Give a five-minute warning so he knows when it's almost time to go.

THE EXPERT: Susan Ginsberg, Ed.D., corporate parenting-education consultant, and publisher of *Work & Family Life* newsletter.

As a child's imagination grows, so can a host of fears. Most eventually disappear on their own. If the fear intensifies and interferes with your child's daily life, seek professional help. Monitor your own reactions to things so your child doesn't pick up on your anxieties.

Common childhood fears

▶ **1-2 years:** dark, thunder and lightning, the bath, toilet training, separation, strangers, animals, and doctors.

▶ **2-3 years:** drains, new situations, dark, dogs, scary noises, monsters, death; plus fear of animals, separation, strangers, and toilet training persist.

▶ **3-4 years:** bad thoughts, loss of control (like bed-wetting), loss of a parent, dark, animals, monsters, and new situations (including day care or school).

▶ **4-5 years:** fears are based more on reality — dogs, sounds (like thunder), getting lost, losing parent.

▶ **5-6 years:** fears intensify and specialize — wild animals, monsters, insects, injury, water, parent's death.

Do . . .

▶ Acknowledge fears without giving them excessive attention. Let your child know that you're there for him.

▶ Help your child put his fears into words or pictures to make them less threatening.

▶ Encourage your child to tackle his own fears by empowering him with confidence and a sense of control. Talk about what he can do to help himself — for example, say a magic word or lock the closet to keep out monsters.

▶ Replace scary mental images with facts: show a child who is afraid of going down the drain how his toy can stay in the tub while the water drains out and nothing happens to it.

▶ Let your child overcome his fear at his own pace.

Don't . . .

▶ Ridicule a child or belittle his fears.

▶ Say, "There's nothing to be afraid of" or "Don't be such a baby." Instead, listen and comfort.

▶ Force children to confront their fears directly before they're ready. It may magnify the problem.

▶ Overprotect your child by avoiding situations completely, or he'll never overcome his fear.

 THE EXPERT: Robert Schachter, psychologist, former director of the Phobia Center for Children, New York, and coauthor of *When Your Child Is Afraid* (Fireside, 1988).

*Discipline
doesn't
just mean
punishment; it
should teach
your child to
follow rules,
respect others,
and learn a
lesson for the
next time.*

Discipline

**It's natural for children to try to break the rules —
they learn by constantly testing limits. And
though they don't realize it, they want you to be
authoritative to help them stay in control.**

**The key to effective discipline is to remember
that no single tactic works all the time or with
every child. Repeating a strategy too often
loses effectiveness.**

▶ Set clear rules so children know
what's expected.

▶ Present a united front with your
spouse or partner.

▶ Make sure the consequences fit the "crime," are
enforceable, and aren't harder on the parents
than on the child. (For example, if your children fight
during dinner, make them leave the table
or eat a cold meal later; don't take
away TV for a month.)

▶ Act quickly and firmly. Don't wait for children to
step-up whining or bargaining before taking
action or caving in to their demands.

▶ Vary the repertoire with a host of techniques,
including time-outs, the star system
and family meetings.

- Don't be afraid to change your mind if you go overboard on a punishment — grounding your child every weekend for a month — and later feel trapped by it. You'll teach your child that it's okay to be reflective on impulsive actions and rethink decisions.

- Don't discuss why your child misbehaved in the heat of the moment. Talk later when everyone is calm.

- Praise good behavior. Children crave attention, but they'll misbehave if that's the only way they get it.

Time-out

Instead of spanking, many parents try the time-out method of removing a child from the scene of his misbehavior to cool off and get his act together. Psychologist James Varni, author of *Time-Out for Toddlers* (Berkley Books, 1991), suggests this method for children over age 2:

- When your child misbehaves, remove him immediately from the situation. Simply tell him what he did wrong and state the preferred behavior.
- If possible, put him in a time-out before his behavior escalates and he's out of control.
- Escort him to a time-out chair in a corner or hallway, away from the action — not in his room.
- Set a timer for one minute for every year of his age.
- When the timer rings, announce, "Time's up." Let your child return to his activity. Do not discuss the problem at that time.

THE EXPERT: Ron Taffel, Ph.D., child and family therapist, and author of *Why Parents Disagree: How We Can Work Together* (William Morrow, 1994).

LEARNING

What to do about stuttering

Stumbling over an occasional word or repeating certain syllables, words or phrases is a normal part of language development that's usually outgrown.

But some children continue to stutter. If your child has a speech disfluency that lasts for more than six months, have him evaluated by a speech-language pathologist. Treating stuttering before it becomes habitual and entrenched can spare your child unnecessary social and emotional problems.

For information, support groups, or the name of a local speech-language pathologist, call the Stuttering Foundation of America: 800-992-9392 or the American Speech-Language-Hearing Association: 800-638-8255.

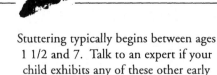

Stuttering typically begins between ages 1 1/2 and 7. Talk to an expert if your child exhibits any of these other early speech problems as well:
• No words by 18 months.
• No intelligible speech by age 2.
• No two-word sentences by age 2 1/2.

The child with a stuttering problem:

▶ Repeats sounds more than twice, li-li-li-li-like this.

▶ Tension and struggle may be evident in the facial muscles, especially around the mouth.

▶ The pitch of the voice may rise with repetitions, and occasionally the child will experience a "block" — no airflow or voice for several seconds.

▶ Severe stuttering occurs when a child stutters more than 10 percent of the time, with considerable effort and tension, or avoids stuttering by changing words and using extra sounds to get started.

How to help a child who stutters

▶ Model slow, relaxed speech when talking with your child and encourage others to do the same, but don't talk so slowly that it sounds abnormal. (Try to sound like Mister Rogers.)

▶ Don't rush your child by interrupting or finishing words for him. Don't let others rush or tease him.

▶ Try not to be upset or annoyed when stuttering increases. Be patient and accepting. Say, "I know it's hard to talk at times, but lots of people get stuck on words; it's okay."

▶ Encourage your child to talk about his stuttering. Overcoming the problem is more a matter of losing the fear of stuttering than of trying harder.

 THE EXPERT: *Stuttering Foundation of America.*

Storytelling can entertain, educate, calm fears, build self-confidence, instill parental values, and bond parent and child.

How to tell a bedtime story

▶ Keep stories short and simple.

▶ Use facial expressions, hand gestures, sound effects and different voices.

▶ Be spontaneous; but when your goal is to communicate a lesson, know how you're going to resolve the story.

▶ Use real life. Children love to hear stories about themselves, how Mom and Dad met, etc.

▶ Create a set of characters who have continuing adventures. Name them after your child and his friends.

▶ Let children participate: they can say the magic words or chant repeating lines.

▶ Have fun; your enthusiasm is contagious.

For books, newsletters and tapes on the art of storytelling, or to find a local storytelling festival, call the National Storytelling Association: 800-525-4514.

THE EXPERT: National Storytelling Association.

Blueprint for a classic bedtime story

Here are the basic blocks on which to build a story:

▶ *Once upon a time* . . . Transports child and parent to a magical place.

▶ *. . . there was a likable hero* . . . Children respond to heroes with concerns and troubles like their own. Choose your child's favorite animal and use descriptive names and qualities: "Busybody the squirrel had chocolate-colored eyes and he never wanted to go to bed."

▶ *. . . who had reason to travel* . . . Use one of your child's emotions — curiosity, fear, loneliness — to motivate your hero to venture into a larger world.

▶ *. . . when a threat occurs* . . . Conflict, whether a snag or an adversary, brings the story excitement and meaning.

▶ *. . . from which there is a hero-inspired way out* . . . Let the hero have a clever idea for escape or victory rather than having him be rescued by a fairy godmother's magic wand.

▶ *. . . which results in a safe return and a happy ending.* The hero has escaped or defeated the threat and returns home, reassuring your child that he, too, can succeed, solve problems, and learn something in the process.

Don't just tell stories at bedtime, tell them in the car, at bathtime, or anytime you have 10 minutes with your children.

THE EXPERT: Chase Collins, author of *Tell Me a Story: Creating Bedtime Tales Your Children Will Dream On* (Houghton Mifflin, 1992).

How to grow a bookworm

▶ Start reading to your child from infancy.

▶ Make reading together a daily family activity.

▶ Continue reading aloud to your child even if he can read by himself.

▶ Introduce a variety of books, including poetry, short stories and nonfiction.

▶ Teach your child to value books: find a special place for them within easy reach; use bookplates to identify the proud owner.

▶ Let your child choose the books he wants to read and add to his collection.

▶ Let your child see you reading for pleasure.

▶ Talk about what you read.

▶ Visit the library regularly.

▶ Give books and magazine subscriptions as gifts.

▶ Bring books to read when you're waiting in lines, at the doctor's office, or anywhere you have time to kill.

▶ Tape-record yourself reading your child's favorite books or buy books on tape so he can read along.

▶ Use television to encourage reading. Get books on people, places and things that interest your child when they're on TV.

▶ Relate books to real life: read books about emotions, events or stages in your child's life.

▶ Make reading part of life: read aloud street signs, cereal boxes, recipes and newspapers.

▶ Put picture/word labels on objects around the house — "chair," "door," "truck" — so your child begins to associate words with meaning.

▶ Connect reading and writing. Encourage your child to write: provide crayons, pens and paper for him to write thank-you notes, grocery lists, and to make his own books.

 THE EXPERT: *International Reading Association.*

Classic books every toddler should know

▶ *Blueberries for Sal*
by Robert McCloskey (Puffin)

▶ *Brown Bear, Brown Bear, What Do You See?*
by Eric Carle (Henry Holt)

▶ *Caps for Sale*
by Esphyr Slobodkina (HarperTrophy)

▶ *Curious George*
by H. A. Rey (Houghton Mifflin)

▶ *The Little Engine That Could*
by Walter Piper (Platt & Munk)

▶ *The Tale of Peter Rabbit*
by Beatrix Potter (Frederick Warne & Co.)

▶ *The Very Hungry Caterpillar*
by Eric Carle (Philomel)

▶ *The Runaway Bunny*
by Margaret Wise Brown (HarperTrophy)

The American Library Association suggests that you occasionally stop and talk about what you're reading. Ask:
"Why does the mouse look afraid?"
"What do you think will happen next?"
"What would you do if you were the prince?"

THE EXPERT: Hannah Nuba, program coordinator, The New York Public Library Early Childhood Resource and Information Center.

Toddler talk timetable

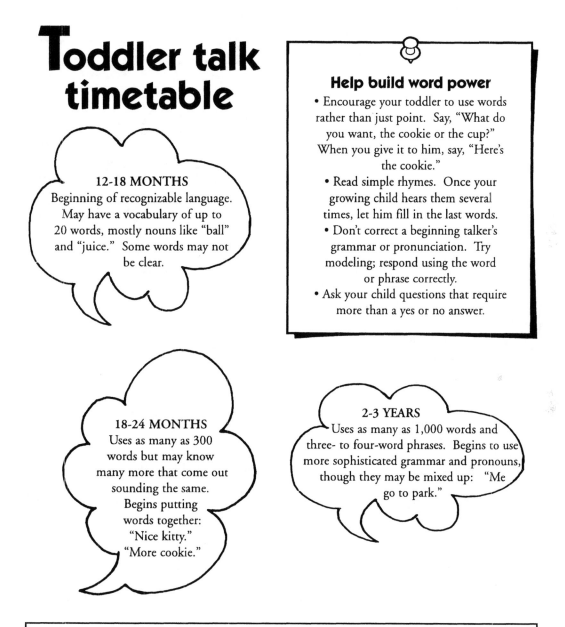

12-18 MONTHS
Beginning of recognizable language. May have a vocabulary of up to 20 words, mostly nouns like "ball" and "juice." Some words may not be clear.

Help build word power
• Encourage your toddler to use words rather than just point. Say, "What do you want, the cookie or the cup?" When you give it to him, say, "Here's the cookie."
• Read simple rhymes. Once your growing child hears them several times, let him fill in the last words.
• Don't correct a beginning talker's grammar or pronunciation. Try modeling; respond using the word or phrase correctly.
• Ask your child questions that require more than a yes or no answer.

18-24 MONTHS
Uses as many as 300 words but may know many more that come out sounding the same. Begins putting words together: "Nice kitty." "More cookie."

2-3 YEARS
Uses as many as 1,000 words and three- to four-word phrases. Begins to use more sophisticated grammar and pronouns, though they may be mixed up: "Me go to park."

THE EXPERT: Naomi Baron, Ph.D., professor of linguistics, American University, Washington, D.C., and author of *Growing Up with Language: How Children Learn to Talk* (Addison-Wesley, 1993).

PLAYING

How to buy toys your child will love

When choosing a toy for your child, keep in mind his age, interests and stage of development. Look for:

▶ Age ranges on toy packages; they're based on a child's physical and mental abilities, plus the safety aspects of a toy.

▶ Toys that do more than one thing or that can be played with in different ways as children grow, like puppets, blocks and dolls.

▶ Simple, unstructured, and open-ended toys to encourage the use of imagination and creativity.

▶ Educational is great, but a toy should be fun first.

▶ Stick to your values. If you don't believe in war toys, explain your beliefs to your child, but don't be surprised if he turns everyday objects into guns and knives.

▶ Recognize the toys your child likes at the doctor's office or other friends' houses.

Questions to ask:

• Is this toy safe for my child's age?
• Does my child have the coordination and attention span required to enjoy it?
• Will my child be interested enough to play with it over and over?
• Will it spark his imagination?
• Can it be used creatively?

Toy box favorites 1-3 years

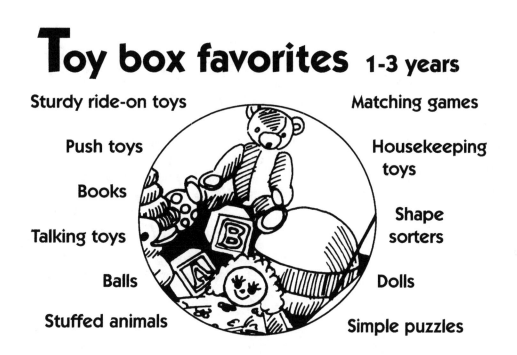

Sturdy ride-on toys

Push toys

Books

Talking toys

Balls

Stuffed animals

Matching games

Housekeeping toys

Shape sorters

Dolls

Simple puzzles

Look for toys that . . .

▶ Provide balance and mobility.

▶ Enhance gross and fine motor skills.

▶ Help memory and build analytical thinking skills.

▶ Encourage role-playing and language development by helping children imitate what they observe in the world around them.

Many major toy companies will replace missing or broken pieces for free or for a small fee. Call the company's consumer affairs department. (Phone numbers are often listed on the box or call the 800 operator.)

THE EXPERT: Helen Boehm, Ph.D., educational psychologist and toy expert, senior vice president at the MTV Network, and author of *The Right Toys* (Bantam Books, 1986).

Your child's squiggles and dots may look like a jumble to you, but to him they may tell a whole story that reveals how he views the world.

Talking to children about their art

How you talk to your child about his creations and the value you place on them can influence his self-esteem and creativity. But getting a budding Michelangelo to talk about his work is a delicate art.

What not to say

▶ "Don't get messy!" A sure way to inhibit an artist. Give your child lots of blank paper and the freedom to experiment.

▶ "Why don't you color the tree green?" There's no right or wrong way to be creative, so don't criticize your child's work or judge the way he's doing it.

▶ "What a beautiful picture." Rather than simple praise, encourage the effort: "You really worked hard making all those colorful circles."

▶ "I'm just making it better." Trying to "fix" your child's picture by adding clouds to the sky can frustrate him and make him doubt his own ability.

What to say

▶ "That's an interesting picture, can you tell me about it?" Or, "Can you tell me the story of your picture?" Don't tell your child what you see, ask him what *he* created.

▶ "Those colors make me feel happy." Comment on the visual elements — shapes, colors, actions and feelings evoked — to emphasize the process, not the end product.

▶ "Those shapes are really swirling around." Use observational rather than judgmental words.

▶ "Black is such a dark color. White is a light color. Look what happened when you mixed them together — you got gray." Make comments that teach.

▶ "You must be proud of that picture." Help your child create to please himself, not you.

▶ "Would you like me to write your name on it and hang it up?" The artwork is his, so get permission before you write on it or display it.

THE EXPERT: Leslie McMahon-Bushara, early childhood coordinator, Children's Museum of Manhattan, New York.

When selecting videos for your child to borrow, rent or buy, do some research and look for those that entertain, educate, appeal to a child's sense of imagination — or offer a combination of these qualities.

Selecting children's videos

▶ Ask your friends or local librarian for suggestions.

▶ Pick videos that are adaptations from favorite books, have won awards, or were produced by companies with a good reputation in the children's video market.

▶ Look for those with some educational value, such as *Sesame Street* characters teaching the alphabet.

▶ If possible, rent a movie first, and if your child loves it and wants to watch it over and over again, then buy it. Or better yet, borrow from your local library video collection — your child can choose a free video with each visit.

Video selections for ages 1-4

▶ *Barney's Campfire Sing-Along*
(Lyons Group Video)

▶ *Mary Poppins*
(Walt Disney Home Video)

▶ *Pre-School Power: Little Kids Doing Big Things*
(Concept Associates)

▶ *Raffi in Concert with the Rise and Shine Band*
(A&M Video)

▶ *Richard Scarry's Best ABC Video Ever*
(Random House Home Video)

▶ *Rugrats* series
(Nickelodeon)

▶ *Shari Lewis Presents 101 Things for Kids to Do*
(A&M Video)

▶ *The Little Engine That Could*
(MCA/Universal)

▶ *The Little Mermaid*
(Walt Disney Home Video)

▶ *Wee Sing series*
(Price, Stern, Sloan)

▶ *Where the Wild Things Are*
(Weston Woods)

 THE EXPERT: Joanna Langfield, movie critic, commentator, and host of the syndicated radio program *Joanna Langfield's Entertainment Reports.*

Chapter Five

PRESCHOOLER
THREE–FIVE YEARS

DAILY CARE

Taking the battle out of bedtime

Children are notorious for the bedtime stall. Some stubbornly refuse to go to bed without a tantrum; others delay going to sleep with requests for "one more" drink, kiss or trip to the bathroom. Here's how to get your child to bed and keep her there.

● Set an appropriate bedtime hour and stick to it.

● Reserve the half hour before bedtime for quiet play to help your child wind down. Avoid stimulating activities.

● Give advance warning one half hour before you want to begin the bedtime routine. Then give a 10-minute warning. Use a timer as an impersonal third party to signal when the 10 minutes are up so you're not the bad guy.

● Firmly announce, "It's time to get ready for bed," and begin the bedtime ritual together.

● Brush teeth, read a story, and say good night to all the stuffed animals. Whatever bedtime routine you create, follow a predictable sequence of events every night.

● If your child protests when you leave, assure her that you will return in five minutes. Tell her that she doesn't have to go to sleep right away, but she can rest quietly in bed.

How to set and enforce limits with a bedtime rebel

● Make bedtime limits positive, impersonal and specific:
Positive: "You can watch one more TV show before bed," instead of, "No more TV after eight o'clock."
Impersonal: "The clock says it's eight o'clock."
Specific: "It's time to get ready for bed — put on your pajamas, brush your teeth, and pick out a book."

● Give a reason and state a consequence:
Reason: "You must go to sleep now so you will feel happy tomorrow."
Consequence: "If you don't call out once you're in bed at eight-thirty I will come back into your room to see how you're doing every 15 minutes. But if you call out I will not answer your questions and the 15-minute wait starts all over again."

● Praise your child's efforts. If she hasn't been listening, tell her you're sorry you couldn't visit the night before because she kept calling out, but you're sure she'll follow the rules better tonight.

According to sleep expert Dr. Richard Ferber, here's how much sleep your preschooler needs:

3 years	12 hours
4 years	11 1/2 hours
5 years	11 hours

THE EXPERT: Charles Schaefer, Ph.D., child psychologist and director of the Better Sleep Clinic at Fairleigh Dickinson University, Hackensack, New Jersey, and coauthor of *Winning Bedtime Battles: How to Help Your Child Develop Good Sleep Habits* (Carol Publishing,

FEEDING

According to the U.S. Department of Agriculture, our daily diet should look like a pyramid — with lots of breads and cereals at the base and only a few fats, oils and sweets at the top.

A child-sized food pyramid

Since young children need less food than adults, cut down on portion size, rather than number of recommended servings. A preschooler's portion is about one quarter to one half of an adult's. (Increase portion size as your child grows.) The opposite chart suggests some child-sized portions for children between the ages of 3 and 6.

Try to serve items from several food groups at every meal. But remember: although children's diets don't always balance out daily, they usually do over several days of healthy eating and snacking.

Breads, cereals, rice and pasta **6-11 servings a day.** **One serving equals:**	• 1/3 to 1/2 cup of cooked pasta or rice • 1/4 cup of dry cereal • 1 mini muffin or 2 graham cracker squares • 1/3 to 1/2 of a sandwich
Fruits **2-4 servings a day.** **One serving equals:**	• 10 grapes • 1/2 an apple • 2-4 ounces of fruit juice • 2 tablespoons of dried fruit
Vegetables **3-5 servings a day.** **One serving equals:**	• 4-5 French fries • 2 broccoli florets • 1/3 ear of corn • 1/3 cup of raw or cooked veggies
Meat, poultry, fish, beans, eggs and nuts **2-3 servings a day.** **One serving equals:**	• 3 chicken nuggets or 1 small drumstick • 1/2 of a 3-oz. hamburger • 1/3 cup of cooked beans • 1-2 tablespoons of peanut butter
Milk, yogurt and cheese **2-3 servings a day.** **One serving equals:**	• 3/4 cup of milk • 1 slice American cheese or 1 string cheese "finger" • 3/4 cup of yogurt or frozen yogurt
Fats, oils and sweets **1 serving a day.** **One serving equals:**	• 1 cookie

 THE EXPERT: Children's Nutrition Research Center, Baylor College of Medicine, Houston.

Selecting the best treats

You may not want to offer sugar-coated cereals for breakfast, but a few handfuls can be a good snack. It's low in fat, high in fiber, and loaded with vitamins and minerals. Plus, it provides a sweet fix that's healthier than the high saturated-fat content of many other treats. Mix with plain cereal or Cheerios.

Here are some healthy alternatives, lower in fat and higher in nutrients, than some usual fare.

Instead of:	Try:
● Ice cream	● Fozen yogurt
● Flavored ices	● Frozen juice pops
● Potato chips	● Pretzels
● Canned fruit	● Fresh or dried fruit
● Fruit punch	● 100 percent fruit juice
● Soda	● Fruit juice and seltzer
● Chocolate cake	● Corn or bran muffin
● Chocolate chip cookies	● Fig bars or graham crackers
● High-fat crackers	● Rice cakes

THE EXPERT: Jo-Ann Heslin, registered dietitian and nutrition consultant, coauthor of *No-Nonsense Nutrition for Kids* (Pocket Books, 1985).

Lunch box fare

If your child brings home a full lunch box or confesses that she's trading with her friends, she may be getting bored with the tried and true. Add a little creativity for delicious meals she won't pass up. Try these combinations and ask your child to suggest some of her own.

- Pair peanut butter with nutritious alternatives to jelly: crushed pineapple, applesauce, sliced banana, flavored yogurt, raisins or diced apple.

- Use cookie cutters to make fun sandwich shapes.

- Send two different sandwich halves.

- Try various breads: English muffins, croissants, pitas, bagels, rice cakes, tortillas, hamburger and hot dog buns.

- Scoop out an orange and fill the round peel with orange-walnut-chicken salad.

- Send raw veggies with a container of dip.

Lunch box fun

- Put a picture message in your child's lunch box.
- Surprise your child with stickers or family photos taped inside the lunch box lid.
- Add a leftover party favor or birthday or holiday-theme napkin.
- Draw a face on a brown paper bag and show your child how to turn her lunch sack into a puppet when she's done eating.

To keep peanut butter and jelly sandwiches from getting soggy, spread a thin layer of peanut butter on both slices of bread; then add a layer of jelly in the middle.

THE EXPERT: Ellen Klavan, nutrition and health writer, author of *The Creative Lunch Box* (Crown, 1991) and *The Vegetarian Fact-Finder* (The Little Bookroom, 1996).

HEALTH

Sometimes it's obvious that you should keep your child home, but other times are debatable. If unsure, err on the side of caution.

Is your child sick enough to stay home?

Always make sure your child is up to going to school, day care or just going out, and check with your pediatrician if you think your child may be contagious. Keep your child home with:

- Temperature higher than 100 degrees Fahrenheit first thing in the morning

- Severe diarrhea

- Repeated vomiting

- Red, watery eyes with yellowish discharge

- Raspy, barking cough (if associated with other symptoms)

- Ear pain (may indicate an infection)

- Unidentified rash or rash accompanied by fever

- Severe headache or abdominal pain

- Painful or frequent urination

- Unusual tiredness or weakness

When you can send your child back to school

With some viral infections, children are most contagious 24 to 48 hours before symptoms even appear. During that time you can't prevent your child from spreading germs. But once symptoms appear, children should be kept home until medical treatment has taken effect and/or they are no longer contagious. Here's when your child should be well enough to return to school:

- Chicken pox: Six to seven days from the onset of the rash, and when all lesions have crusted over (but not necessarily fallen off).

- Conjuctivitis: When redness clears and there is no leakage from the eyes; about 48 hours after beginning antibiotic eyedrops.

- Fever: After being fever free for 24 hours (in the absence of any other symptoms).

- Lice: Once hair is treated and all nits are removed.

- Measles: Seven days after rash appears.

- Strep throat: 24 hours after beginning antibiotics.

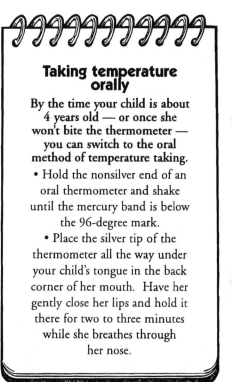

Taking temperature orally

By the time your child is about 4 years old — or once she won't bite the thermometer — you can switch to the oral method of temperature taking.

• Hold the nonsilver end of an oral thermometer and shake until the mercury band is below the 96-degree mark.

• Place the silver tip of the thermometer all the way under your child's tongue in the back corner of her mouth. Have her gently close her lips and hold it there for two to three minutes while she breathes through her nose.

THE EXPERT: Donald Schiff, M.D., pediatrician; past president of the American Academy of Pediatrics, professor of pediatrics at the University of Colorado Medical School, Denver.

Between ages 5 and 7, baby teeth begin to loosen and fall out as the permanent ones arrive. The process continues until age 11 or 12.

Teeth

Heredity plays a major role in when baby teeth fall out, but *how* they fall out usually follows a pattern.

● The normal sequence for teeth to fall out is for the lower two incisors (center teeth) to fall out first. The upper two incisors follow.

● Symmetry is important in dental growth and tooth loss — if the left tooth falls out first, it should be followed by the right (or vice versa). If there is a delay of longer than six months between the loss of one tooth and the corresponding tooth, check with your dentist.

● When your child has a loose tooth, it's best to let it fall out on its own. If your child inadvertently swallows one it will pass right through the digestive system.

● If you want to help a very loose tooth fall out, let your child chew a piece of sugarless bubble gum. The tooth should be out painlessly in minutes.

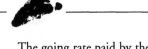

The going rate paid by the tooth fairy is currently about $1.50 per tooth, according to Rosemary Wells, tooth fairy consultant and founder of the Tooth Fairy Museum in Deerfield, Illinois.

That's up from 35 cents in the 1950s and one dollar in the early 1980s.

Make toothbrushing fun

By age 3 you can teach your child how to brush her teeth by herself. Continue to supervise brushing and go over the teeth yourself until age 6 or 7, when children have the dexterity and determination to do a thorough job. Encourage children to brush for about two minutes.

- Let your child choose her own toothbrush and flavored fluoride toothpaste.

- Play a game of "You start, I finish," to make sure no teeth are missed.

- Brush together, playing "Monkey see, monkey do," so your child imitates you.

- Brush your child's teeth while she brushes yours.

- Use a musical toothbrush or set a timer or a music box and brush until it stops.

Hold that tooth

- If your child breaks, chips or knocks out a tooth, contact a dentist immediately.
- A baby tooth will not be replaced, but a dentist may insert a space retainer to save room for the permanent tooth.
- A permanent tooth can be reattached if you act quickly. Handle the tooth gently by the crown, not the root.
- Either reinsert the tooth in its socket and have your child hold it in place by biting down on a clean piece of gauze; put the tooth in a glass of milk or water, or wrap it in a wet cloth. And get to the dentist's office fast.

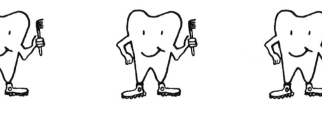

 THE EXPERT: American Academy of Pediatric Dentistry.

Unlike problems that cause pain, children rarely complain about their eyesight. They may not be seeing clearly, but they don't know there's any other way to see.

How to spot a vision problem

The American Optometric Association recommends that eye exams be given at ages 3 and 5 and then annually. Most vision problems can be treated with corrective lenses or vision therapy. Warning signs for your preschooler or school-age child:

- Fatigue, headache, nausea or dizziness after reading or doing close work.

- Dislikes or avoids close work; has short attention span for such work; frequently daydreams.

- Sits too close to the television; prefers reading or other close work to sports and outdoor games.

- Difficulty reading or unusual posture or behavior during reading, including covering one eye or using a finger to follow text.

- Difficulties in school. (Your child may not be able to see clearly.)

Reading by flashlight under the covers won't cause your child any permanent eye damage; only temporary eye fatigue.

THE EXPERT: American Optometric Association.

If your child needs glasses

● Let your child choose her own frames; if she likes them, she'll wear them.

● Choose shatter-resistant polycarbonate plastic lenses and ask for a scratch-proof coating.

● Make sure they fit comfortably.

● Teach your child proper cleaning, handling and storing methods.

● Encourage a positive attitude about glasses so your child wears them with a smile.

How to protect your child's eyes

● Buy an antireflection filter screen to mute computer glare. Keep computers out of direct sunlight or fluorescent lighting.

● Make sure your child wears appropriate protective helmets, face masks and goggles during sports activities.

● Avoid dangerous toys like bows and arrows, darts, BB guns, and anything with points, rods, sharp edges or projectiles.

● Do not allow children to handle spray dispensers.

Buying sunglasses

Protect your child's eyes from the sun's harmful rays with a good pair of sunglasses. Look for those that say "100 percent UV protection" or "Meets ANSI (American National Standards Institute) UV requirements." Even inexpensive sunglasses can provide good protection. Look for amber, gray or green lenses; pink, yellow and blue may not screen out glare as well.

THE EXPERT: Better Vision Institute.

Head lice is the most common communicable childhood disease. All children are susceptible no matter how often they shampoo or bathe.

Lice advice

The most common way to be infected with lice is through direct contact with someone who has it, or by sharing combs, brushes or headwear.

- Itching is the first sign of infestation. Check your child's scalp, behind the ears, and the back of the neck.

- Lice move quickly, so what you'll see are nits — tiny, pale gray, oval-shaped eggs "glued" at an angle to the hair shaft. (Nits are often mistaken for dandruff; dandruff will come off with the flick of a finger, nits will not.)

- If a family member is infested, check everyone in your household. Notify your child's school and playmates.

- Ask your pediatrician or pharmacist to recommend a pesticidal hair product. (Inform them if your child has allergies or if anyone in your house is pregnant or nursing.) The National Pediculosis Association advises against using any product that contains lindane, often recognized by the brand name Kwell.)

- Treat only those who are infested. Do not use chemical treatments as a preventive measure, or on infested eyebrows or eyelashes. Do not treat children under age 2 without consulting a doctor.

- After treatment, you need to physically remove any remaining nits with a nit removal comb, blunt safety scissors or your fingernails.

- Wash all bedding, recently worn clothing, and headwear in hot water and put in a hot dryer.

- Vacuum upholstery, mattresses, pillows, rugs, stuffed animals and car seats where nits may be located.

- Soak combs, brushes and hair accessories in hot — not boiling — water for 10 minutes.

Avoid the spread of lice

- Store hats in coat sleeves instead of hanging on common hooks.

- Don't pile coats on top of each other.

- Braid or pin up long, loose hair.

- Have children use their own nap mats and store separately.

- Don't share combs, brushes, hair accessories, hats or headphones.

- Remove headwear from school dress-up areas.

Lice are small, wingless insects the size of sesame seeds that feed on human blood.

THE EXPERT: *National Pediculosis Association.*

SAFETY

How to crimeproof your children

- As soon as they are able, help children memorize their full name, address, phone number and how to call 911 or the operator in an emergency.

- Teach them how to get help. Point out safe people (store clerk, firefighter) and safe havens (library, a friend's house).

- Play "what-if" role-playing games to rehearse situations that might arise and how to handle them. "What if a stranger offered you candy?" "What if we were separated at the mall?"

- Explain that a "stranger" doesn't have to be a scary-looking man, but is anyone your children or you don't know, including friendly teenagers or women. Teach children they should never go anywhere with or take anything from a stranger.

- Establish a family code word. Tell your children not to go with someone who says, "Your mother sent me to get you," unless that person says the code. Rehearse it.

- Don't make children easy targets by visibly displaying their names on clothing or book bags.

- Be a role model. Practice your own good security measures: Always ask who's at the door before opening it; lock car doors, etc.

- As older children go off without you, teach them to stay with a buddy, avoid isolated areas, and remain in public view. Get to know the parents of your children's friends and find out who will be home during play dates.

- Write down and discuss safety rules with your caregiver.

- Keep communication open so your children feel free to tell you if something or someone is bothering them. Teach them to trust their instincts.

 THE EXPERT: J. L. Simmons, Ph.D., social psychologist and crime prevention expert, coauthor of *76 ways to Protect Your Child from Crime* (Henry Holt, 1992).

Halloween safety

- Choose safe costumes: light-colored, not oversized, and no high heels or large, floppy shoes. Attach hats and wigs securely.

- Use makeup or nontoxic face paint instead of masks. If a mask is a must, enlarge eyeholes to make it easier for child to see.

- Make sure props, like swords and knives, are made out of flexible plastic or cardboard.

- Put reflective tape or stickers on costumes and goody bags. Provide flashlights.

- Make sure young children are supervised by an adult or responsible older child. Review traffic safety rules.

- Have children stay in a group, stick to familiar neighborhoods and well-lit houses, and never enter anyone's home.

- Tell children not to eat any treats until they're brought home and inspected. (Feed children before they go, or let them sample your goodies first, so they'll be less tempted.) When in doubt, throw it out.

Instead of giving only sweet treats to trick-or-treaters, hand out rubber spiders, colorful pencils, stickers or washable tattoos.

THE EXPERT: National Safety Council.

Fire safety

- Never leave children unattended with a lit candle, fireplace, barbecue, stove or any open flame.

- Teach children that matches and lighters are not toys. Keep them locked and out of reach.

- Design a fire escape plan with two ways out of every room. Practice at least twice a year.

What to teach children

- Stay away from hot things that can hurt. Tell a grown-up if you find matches or lighters.

- Run cool water on a burn.

- Know the warning sound of the smoke detector/alarm.

- If a fire starts, do not hide; get out of the house fast and go where you can be seen and rescued.

- If clothes catch on fire, stop; cover your face with your hands; drop to the floor, and roll.

- Crawl low under smoke, covering mouth, nose and eyes. Do not open a hot door — there may be fire on the other side.

- Do not stop for toys or pets, or go back in for anything.

- Know that firefighters are helpers.

THE EXPERT: National Fire Protection Association.

How to buy a bicycle for your child

- Buy a bike that fits your child now, not one she has to grow into.

- A bike fits when your child can place both feet flat on the ground while seated. When standing astride a bike with a top bar, there should be a clearance of 1 to 1 1/2 inches between the crotch and the bar.

- When seated, handlebars should be about waist high.

- Make sure the steel bracing bar between the handlebars is padded.

- Choose a single-speed model with coaster or foot brakes. Hand brakes are too difficult for young children.

How to teach your child to ride a two-wheeler

Children need balance and coordination to ride a two-wheeler without training wheels. They may be ready between the ages of 5 and 7.

● Try teaching your child to ride on dirt or grass — it's harder to ride on but softer to fall on.

● Make sure the seat is low enough so your child can steady herself by resting her feet on the ground.

● Slightly raise training wheels so they no longer touch the ground when your child is riding, but keep her from falling when her balance waivers.

● While your child pedals, run alongside holding onto the back of the seat and the handlebars. When your child begins to balance, let go of the handlebars; then release the seat.

> Teach children an important rule of the road: Walk against traffic; ride with traffic.

THE EXPERT: Bicycle Federation of America.

How to choose a bicycle helmet

Research shows that bicycle helmets reduce the risk of head injury by 85 percent, yet most children don't wear them regularly.

Accidents can happen even in your driveway, so teach your child to always wear a helmet. Set an example by wearing your own. Let your child choose a helmet she likes so she'll wear it. Look for:

- **An approval sticker from the Consumer Product Safety Commission or the SNELL Memorial Foundation certifying that the helmet meets safety standards.**

- **Reflective trim and a bright or white color for greater visibility.**

- **Proper fit, so the helmet sits level and covers the head and the top of the forehead. Try on several models and adjust sizing pads.**

- **Easily adjustable straps. The helmet should be snug, moving only slightly if pushed from side to side, or front to back.**

- **Ventilation vents, since foam holds in heat.**

Car seat safety

According to SafetyBeltSafe
U.S.A.:

- Children who have outgrown car seats should use a safety belt-positioning booster seat till they're about 60 pounds.
    If their heads reach over the top of the backseat while sitting in the booster, choose a booster with a high back.
- For older children using safety belts alone, shoulder belts should fit across the chest, not neck or face. (Never put a shoulder belt under a child's arm.) Lap belts should fit snugly across the top of thighs and lower hips and not ride up on the abdomen. If the belt doesn't lie correctly, the child should use a belt-positioning booster.

☞ THE EXPERT: Bicycle Helmet Safety Institute.

School bus safety

Whether your children ride a bus daily or occasionally on field trips, teach them bus and traffic safety rules:

- Never reach under a bus to retrieve something.

- Never play on the side of the road when getting on or off a bus. Watch for traffic when disembarking.

- Wait for the driver's signal before crossing in front of a bus. Always cross at least 10 feet in front so you can maintain eye contact with the driver.

- If the bus has seat belts, always buckle up.

To make sure your child's school bus is safe, find out:

- How qualified are the drivers? Some states require background checks, drug and alcohol testing, and training reviews; others have no special requirements.

- Who's in charge on the buses? Some districts pay monitors to ride along; others use parents, and some depend on the driver to keep order.

- What type of buses and safety devices are used? Buses should have been built after 1977 when strict federal standards were enacted. Make sure the fleet is well maintained, regularly inspected, and has up-to-date safety features.

Although millions of children travel safely on school buses, every year 50-70 children are killed and more than 10,000 are injured as passengers or when they're getting on or off school buses.

THE EXPERT: National Coalition for School Bus Safety.

191

COPING

How to boost your child's self-esteem

There's a lifelong benefit to helping your child develop a positive self-image at an early age. Here's how to help your child feel good about herself:

- Accept your child for who she is, not what you want her to be.

- Discover and encourage your child's strengths.

- Give your child responsibilities so she feels valued.

- Give her choices to show you trust her decisions.

- Don't solve all her problems; ask for her solutions.

- Help your child learn from her mistakes.

- Encourage independence and self-sufficiency.

- Teach self-discipline: let older children participate in setting household rules and consequences.

- Teach your child to appreciate herself; say, "You must be really proud of yourself."

- Spend time alone with your child and tell her, "You're important to me."

- Make your child feel special through constant encouragement, love and attention.

The National PTA suggests giving your child an empty can labeled "My 'I CAN' Can." Whenever your child learns a new skill — academic, artistic, athletic, etc. — write it on a piece of paper and put it in the can. Review the contents periodically and watch your child's self-esteem soar.

 THE EXPERT: Robert Brooks, Ph.D., psychologist; director of the Department of Psychology, McLean Hospital, Belmont, Massachusetts, and author of *The Self-Esteem Teacher* (American

Although the children's ditty goes, "Sticks and stones will break your bones but words will never hurt me," in fact, words can sometimes be more devastating than actions.

What you should never say to your children

- *"Why can't you be more like your sister?"* Unfavorable comparisons lower self-esteem.

- *"You do that much better than your brother."* Favorable comparisons create competition, fueling rivalry.

- *"Sally is the athlete in the family; James is the artist."* Labeling traps children into roles.

- *"You always make a mess."* Use "I" not "you" statements to criticize the behavior, not the child: "I don't like seeing your toys on the kitchen table."

- *"If you don't pick up your toys you won't get a treat."* More effective: "As soon as you put away your toys we can get ice cream."

● *"I'm leaving without you."*
Don't heighten a child's natural fear of abandonment. Give a five-minute warning so your child has time to get ready.

● *"You don't really hate your brother."*
Don't dismiss negative feelings, acknowledge them: "It seems you have two feelings about your brother; sometimes you like him, and at other times he makes you angry."

● *"I told you so."*
That undermines your child's trust in herself. Substitute, "I can see you wish it had turned out differently."

● *"You never clean up after yourself."*
Avoid sweeping pronouncements that convey a permanent problem. Stick to what needs to be done now: "Garbage goes in the pail."

● *"If you do that one more time . . ."*
Some children view this threat as a challenge to try it "one more time." Instead, offer a choice: "No drumming on the dog's head. You can drum on your drum or on this old pot. You decide."

 THE EXPERT: Adele Faber, sibling relationship expert; coauthor of *Siblings Without Rivalry* (Avon, 1987) and *How to Talk so Kids Will Listen and Listen so Kids Will Talk* (Avon, 1980).

It's important to talk about the death of a pet, friend, or relative openly and honestly with children, being sensitive to their age and level of understanding.

How to discuss death

- The younger the child, the simpler the explanation.

- Use the correct vocabulary, not euphemisms.

- Tell the truth.

- Encourage questions and expect them to continue to arise over time.

- Be available to listen. Acknowledge your child's fears, sadness and loss.

- If your child seems puzzled, ask her what she thinks "dead" means and clear up any confusion.

- Reassure your child that nothing she did, said or thought caused the death. A child who said she wished Grandma was dead may hold herself responsible.

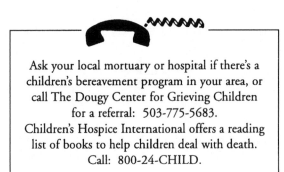

Ask your local mortuary or hospital if there's a children's bereavement program in your area, or call The Dougy Center for Grieving Children for a referral: 503-775-5683.
Children's Hospice International offers a reading list of books to help children deal with death. Call: 800-24-CHILD.

● Allow your child to be angry at the deceased. It's okay if your child says, "I'm angry at Grandpa because we told him to stop smoking and he got lung cancer." Let your child know that you're angry, too.

● Show your emotions. Crying or talking about your grief demonstrates that it's appropriate behavior.

● Discuss any religious beliefs about what happens after death, but you can also say, "Nobody knows for sure."

What not to say about death

● "Grandma went to sleep." Linking death and sleep may make your child fear bedtime.

● "God took Daddy because he was a good man." That may upset a child who thinks that God punishes goodness.

● "Grandpa went on a long trip." Children will wonder why Grandpa didn't say good-bye and will expect him back.

● "Now that Daddy is gone, you'll have to take care of Mommy." Don't put too much responsibility on a young child.

You can start discussing life and death with a young child who notices a dead bug on the windowsill or a dead bird in the park. Explain that no living thing lasts forever. Tell your child to feel her heart and the breath coming out of her nose. Say that the bird's heart doesn't beat and it has stopped breathing. Then explain that when people die they no longer grow, eat or sleep. We don't see them again, but we can keep them alive in our memories and think and talk about them.

THE EXPERT: The Dougy Center for Grieving Children.

When a pet dies

You can deal with the death of a pet in similar ways to other types of death. Also:

- Explain that pets aren't expected to live as long as humans; dogs can live 15 years, but hamsters and guinea pigs usually live only about three.

- If a pet is ill or aging, prepare your child "for the day Buster won't be around anymore." Talk about how to say good-bye.

- Read books about losing a pet.

- If you decide on euthanasia, explain that the veterinarian is going to help the animal die gently so it won't have to feel any more pain. Don't say you're going to put the pet to sleep.

- Don't say the dog ran away; your child may keep waiting for it to come home.

- Help your child grieve. Let your child write a poem or have a memorial service.

- Give your child time to grieve. Don't rush to buy a new pet; that can diminish the special relationship your child had with her pet.

For support in learning how to help your child deal with the loss of a pet, call these pet loss support hotlines:
- University of California, Davis: 916-752-4200
- Michigan State College of Veterinary Medicine: 517-432-2696

 THE EXPERT: Pet Loss Support Hotline, University of California, Davis, School of Veterinary Medicine.

Helping a lefty

Whether your child is left- or right-handed is up to genetics. Trying to force a child to be one or the other can result in emotional problems.

Allow a hand preference to emerge naturally — it's usually established between the ages of 3 and 6.

Until a preference emerges

● Don't pick sides. Throw a ball alternately to each hand.

● Place utensils at the top of the plate and let your child choose which hand to use.

● Don't automatically place a crayon or pencil in your child's right hand.

● Realize that a lefty may still use her right hand for some tasks.

If a left-hand preference emerges

● Buy left-hand scissors, baseball mitts, etc.

● Check that your child doesn't get a right-hand desk at school.

● To teach skills like how to tie a shoelace, a right-handed parent should face a left-handed child so she can mirror your actions.

● Make sure your young southpaw doesn't feel odd or clumsy because she's different or if some things in the right-hand world are difficult for her.

About 15 percent of the population is born left-handed.

THE EXPERT: Lefthanders International, Inc.

199

Sleep disorders

Nightmares and night terrors are two very different sleep disturbances that may be hard to tell apart but need to be responded to differently.

Nightmares

- Can occur at any age and for many reasons.

- Usually occur very late in the sleep period.

- If your child wakes up because of a nightmare, she'll probably need some physical comfort and reassurance.

- Help her separate her nightmare from reality by saying, "It was only a dream. Mommy's here."

- Offer a drink of water and stay with her until she falls back to sleep.

- She may remember the nightmare and want to discuss it the next day. Reassure her that it wasn't real.

Night terrors

● Occur during a partial awakening from the deepest phase of nondreaming sleep; usually within the first few hours after falling sleep.

● Often run in families and can be triggered by overtiredness.

● Are most common between 3 and 7 years.

● A child having a night terror may suddenly scream, cry or thrash about in a confused way. Her eyes may be open, but she isn't awake.

● Parents should not try to rouse or soothe a child as they would during a nightmare; it may only agitate her. Your child may be disoriented and may even push you away.

● Stay calm and make sure your child doesn't hurt herself or sleepwalk. If she gets out of bed, gently steer her back. She'll probably return to an undisturbed sleep within a few minutes.

● Children usually have no memory of such episodes.

 THE EXPERT: Dr. Jamie Whyte, associate director, Sleep Disorders Center at Columbia Presbyterian Medical Center, New York.

Bed-wetting (or enuresis) is usually a physical condition that is often outgrown.

Bed-wetting

Bed-wetting can be treated with behavior modification, bladder control exercises, moisture alarms, medication and other techniques. See your pediatrician to rule out diabetes or urinary tract infections. Other causes for bed-wetting include heredity, a small bladder, deep sleep patterns, and a deficiency of the hormone that decreases urine output during sleep.

● Most children stop wetting their beds by age 4 or 5, although they may have occasional accidents.

● Talk to your pediatrician or see an enuresis specialist if your child has never been able to stay dry overnight by age 6 or 7; was once able to stay dry, but has begun bed-wetting again; has bowel movements or wets her pants during the day, or if the problem is causing emotional stress or low self-esteem at any age.

● While treating the problem, be patient and supportive. Children who are teased or punished for wetting their beds can develop psychological or behavioral problems.

● Help your child cope with embarrassment by planning sleepovers at your house or supplying disposable pads for overnight visits away from home.

For information on bed-wetting treatments, call National Enuresis Society: 800-NES-8080. National Kidney Foundation: 800-622-9010.

THE EXPERT: National Enuresis Society.

Teaching telephone skills

Good telephone manners can save embarrassment, crossed signals and lost messages. Proper use can also be the difference between life and death in an emergency. Start telephone training children around age 3, explaining that the phone is a tool, not a toy.

- If 911 is the emergency number in your area, affix those numbers to all phones. If not, circle 0 for the operator with red nail polish so it stands out.

- Teach children to answer the phone: "Hello. Jones residence. This is Tommy."

- Keep paper and pencils by every phone to encourage children who can write to take messages.

- Advise children, "Don't yell, go tell," so you find out who's calling and the caller's eardrums aren't shattered.

- Rehearse appropriate telephone responses. Explain that the caller doesn't need to know everything (when Mommy's in the bathroom). Tell children to say, "Mommy can't come to the phone right now, may I take a message please?"

- Teach children their phone numbers in pairs — 87-44-39-0. It's easier to remember two numbers at a time.

To have an uninterrupted telephone conversation:

- Keep coloring books, crayons and blocks near the phone so you can play with your child while you talk.
- Give your child a toy phone she can use when you are on the real one.
- Set a timer so your child knows when your call will end.
- Try not to take calls during special family times like meals and storytime. Turn on your answering machine and return calls when your child is sleeping or involved in something.

THE EXPERT: Nancy Friedman, the Telephone "Doctor," telephone skills educator and producer of the video *Telephone Tips for Kids* (Telephone "Doctor").

When you have more than one child, sibling rivalry is inevitable. At the root is each child's desire for the exclusive love of her parents. But there are ways to reduce rivalry.

Sibling rivalry solutions

- Avoid comparisons. Treat each child as an individual and spend time alone with each of them.

- Create cooperative not competitive activities. Instead of pitting children against each other — "Who can make her bed the fastest?" — set shared goals — "Can you work together and make both beds in five minutes?"

- Don't referee every fight. Unless they are hurting each other, let children settle their own arguments. (Young children may need more intervention.)

- Help children verbalize their feelings: "It made you angry when Jeffrey took your toy. You want him to know that he should ask first."

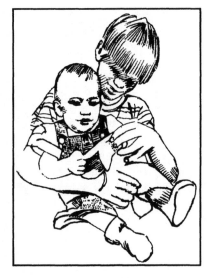

- Help preschoolers settle their disputes by suggesting options: "We can set the timer and take turns playing with the truck or you can figure out a way to play with it together — one loads, the other dumps."

- Set clear rules: "No name-calling. Tell your sister what bothers you without calling her names."

- Try not to play favorites, but also don't worry about always being fair and treating your children equally. Love your children "uniquely," and give attention according to need.

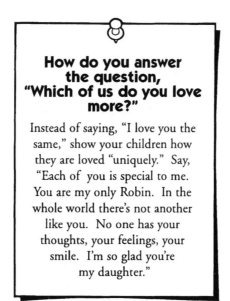

How do you answer the question, "Which of us do you love more?"

Instead of saying, "I love you the same," show your children how they are loved "uniquely." Say, "Each of you is special to me. You are my only Robin. In the whole world there's not another like you. No one has your thoughts, your feelings, your smile. I'm so glad you're my daughter."

THE EXPERT: Adele Faber, sibling relationship expert; coauthor of *Siblings Without Rivalry* (Avon, 1987), and *How to Talk so Kids Will Listen and Listen so Kids Will Talk* (Avon, 1980).

Travel

Before you go

● Talk about the trip in terms children understand.

● Read library books about your destination.

● Ask the local tourism office to send maps and brochures to familiarize your children with what to expect.

What to bring

● Let children pack their favorite books, tapes, toys and security objects in their own backpacks.

● Bring headphones, extra batteries, music and story tapes.

● Pack a surprise bag with coloring books, stickers, audiotapes, magnetic games and special treats to be doled out along the way.

● Choose unbreakable toys. Avoid those with little pieces and those that make noise. Note: Colorforms stick on car, airplane and train windows.

● Bring wipe-and-write or magnetized boards with magnetic letters or numbers.

KidsPorts

Several airports have special play areas for kids:

• Denver International Airport, Colorado
• Pittsburgh International Airport, Pennsylvania
• Boston's Logan Airport, Massachusetts
• San Jose International, California
• Missoula International, Montana
• LaGuardia Airport, New York City

Air travel tips

- Sign up ticketed children for frequent flyer miles.

- Some families choose bulkhead seats for the extra legroom, but remember, there's no storage space for carry-on luggage and armrests don't raise for naps. Instead, try the back of the plane near the flight attendants' station for quick access to bathrooms, drinks and meals.

- Reserve aisle and window seats and you may get the middle seat, too.

- Request kids' meals at least 24 hours in advance.

- Many airlines offer free playing cards, puzzles, magazines and in-flight radio stations featuring children's programming. Ask your flight attendant what's available.

- If you're traveling on a child's birthday, ask about a birthday cake. Some airlines supply one at no charge.

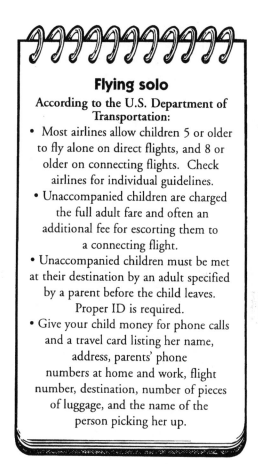

Flying solo

According to the U.S. Department of Transportation:

- Most airlines allow children 5 or older to fly alone on direct flights, and 8 or older on connecting flights. Check airlines for individual guidelines.
- Unaccompanied children are charged the full adult fare and often an additional fee for escorting them to a connecting flight.
- Unaccompanied children must be met at their destination by an adult specified by a parent before the child leaves. Proper ID is required.
- Give your child money for phone calls and a travel card listing her name, address, parents' phone numbers at home and work, flight number, destination, number of pieces of luggage, and the name of the person picking her up.

THE EXPERT: Dorothy Jordon, editor and publisher of *Family Travel Times Newsletter.*

Car survival tips

- Leave right before naptime or bedtime so children sleep en route.

- Keep the backseat clean: cover it with a towel or sheet and then attach car seats.

- Cover metal safety belt and car seat buckles when you park in the sun to protect against burning.

- Keep a ball, Frisbee or jump rope accessible for exercise at rest stops.

- Avoid "are we there yet?" questions: give children their own map and markers. Help them trace the route marking planned stops and estimated arrival times.

- Avoid backseat bickering: before you leave discuss how your children will handle any disagreements. If one arises, read off their own solutions and ask for their cooperation in dealing with it.

Car games

- Make edible necklaces by stringing Cheerios on dental floss or long licorice whips before you go. Make eating a game: you can eat one every five miles or whenever you pass a blue car.
- Look for letters and numbers on road signs and license plates.
- Keep a record of all the state license plates you see.
- Play "I Spy" — take turns picking an object and giving clues until everyone else "spies" it, too.
- Make your own car bingo game: cut out or draw pictures of road signs, vehicles and objects you pass on the road; glue several on cardboard, and cover with clear contact paper. Use wipe-off markers or stickers to mark what you spot. The first person to spot everything on her card wins. Switch cards and play again.

THE EXPERT: Dorothy Jordon, editor and publisher of *Family Travel Times Newsletter.*

How to prevent motion sickness

● Avoid large meals just prior to and during trips.

● Give frequent drinks of fruit juice or soda.

● Keep vehicle cool and well ventilated.

● Have your child focus on the horizon out the front window instead of looking at rushing scenery out the side.

● Don't read or color; sing songs or listen to tapes.

● Make frequent stops and let your child walk around.

● Ask your pediatrician about anti-motion-sickness medication.

● For accidents, carry an extra set of clothes for child and parent, wipes, towel, deodorizer and plastic bags.

When you're on vacation, write your child's name and the hotel or phone number where you're staying on a sticker and put it somewhere inside her clothing in case you get separated.

THE EXPERT: Karl Neumann, M.D., New York City pediatrician and editor of *Traveling Healthy* newsletter.

If you're off on a trip for business or pleasure without the children, don't pack a lot of guilt. Prepare yourself and your children for the separation. Discuss the routine so they know what to expect while you're gone.

When Mom and Dad go out of town

Before you leave

- Tell young children your plans only a few days before. Give older children more time.

- Explain the length of separation in terms children understand: "I'll be home after your next gym class."

- Demystify your trip: leave a map, hotel brochure and a copy of your schedule.

- Mail a postcard home before you leave.

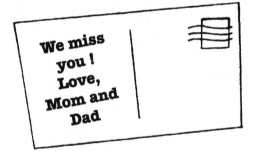

We miss you! Love, Mom and Dad

While you're gone

● Leave an edible calendar: fill a jar with candy, cookies, or favorite treats, with one for each day you'll be away. Your children can eat one each day until you return.

● Hide a series of notes and leave clues for each day.

● Record yourself telling your children's favorite bedtime story or singing a good-night song.

● Call home every day at the same time. Talk first to the adult in charge to get "clued in" about what's happening in your children's lives so you can ask specific questions. Be prepared: your children may not want to talk.

● Have the person watching your children maintain daily rituals, but allow some special treats.

● If you miss a school play or sports event your child is in, have someone videotape it. Watch it together when you return.

When you return

● Spend time with your children before unpacking, but be prepared for the cold shoulder. Give them time to reconnect.

● Elaborate gifts are unnecessary. Souvenirs like postcards, hotel toiletries, or other tokens of your trip show you were thinking about your children.

 THE EXPERT: Susan Ginsberg, Ed.D., corporate parenting-education consultant, and publisher of *Work & Family Life* newsletter.

LEARNING

If you suspect your child has a learning disability, talk to your pediatrician and seek professional help. Once a problem is identified and dealt with, many children with disabilities can function normally.

How to detect learning disabilities

The symptoms of learning disabilities are a diverse set of characteristics that affect development and achievement. Some of these can be found in all children at some time during their development; however, a child with learning disabilities has a cluster of symptoms that do not disappear as she gets older. Many of these children have a hard time absorbing, recalling, retaining, using and expressing information, although they may have average or above-average intelligence.

- Learning Disabilities Association of America: 412-341-1515
- National Center for Learning Disabilities: 212-545-7510

Signs to watch for:

- Short attention span

- Lack of persistence at tasks

- Poor memory

- Difficulty following directions

- Inability to discriminate between letters, numerals or sounds

- Poor reading ability

- Eye-hand coordination problems

- Difficulty with sequencing, telling time and distinguishing right from left

- Delayed or immature speech

- Illegible or inconsistent writing

- Saying one thing and meaning another

- Poor coordination

- Discipline problems

 THE EXPERT: Learning Disabilities Association of America.

*If you think
your child is
gifted, ask your
pediatrician
or local school
board how
to have
her tested.*

How to tell if your child is gifted

Parents often think their children are gifted, and many children are gifted in one area or another. But highly gifted and talented children can function significantly above age level in language development, cognitive and social skills, physical adaptability, and/or creativity.

If your child is exceptionally bright, she may need special challenges and attention to help her reach her potential and prevent her from getting bored with regular classroom work.

Behaviors that may indicate a gifted child:

- An advanced, unusually large vocabulary

- Reads easily or early

- A questioning attitude

- Enjoys problem solving; thinks critically

- Keen powers of observation

- Long attention span; intense concentration

- Unusually good memory

- Wide range of interests or very narrow interests

- Shows creativity or originality in putting ideas and things together in novel ways

- Vivid imagination

- Demonstration of advanced reasoning skills

- Unusual, highly developed sense of humor

- Ability to see relationships and make connections

- Sensitivity and empathy for others

- High energy level

- Independence

- Tends to want older friends

- Intense and sensitive; sometimes a perfectionist

• The Council for Exceptional Children: 800-328-0272
• Gifted Child Society: 201-444-6530, or their Parents Information Network for the Gifted: 900-773-PING
• National Association for Gifted Children: 202-785-4268

THE EXPERT: The Council for Exceptional Children.

If the usual answer to your daily query of "What did you do in school today?" is "Nothing," it may be time to start asking your child in a different way.

How to talk to your child

● Wait to ask questions at the "prime times of communication" when conversations happen naturally — in the car, doing chores together, during a bath, or at bedtime.

● Ask open-ended questions, rather than ones that can be answered with yes or no.

● Investigate the classroom, learn your child's schedule, and get to know her classmates so you can ask specific questions that can generate discussion: "What programs did you work on in computer class?" "What did David bring for show-and-tell?"

● Start talking about your day; it may inspire your child.

● If you don't get a response when you try to initiate a conversation, try again later.

● Don't always make conversation an interrogation or rush to offer advice and criticism.

● Know when not to talk. Read nearby when your child is playing or play with her; she'll open up when she's ready.

216

Conversation starters

- "I noticed when I picked you up that . . ."

- "Do you remember the time you . . . ?"

- "What was the best/silliest thing that happened to you today?"

- "You look as though you feel sad/angry/happy . . ."

- (Use humor) "I heard there was a big, hairy gorilla in your classroom today and he ate everyone's lunch."

Conversation stoppers

- "Why are you always so . . .?"

- "Did you forget your . . . again?"

- "Why don't you ever tell me what's happening at school? Is there something I should know about?"

Young children ask lots of questions, chief among them, "Why?" Instead of simply giving an answer, help your child think for herself by responding, "Why do you think?" This also tells you what your child already knows and helps you determine an appropriate answer.

 THE EXPERT: Raymond Guarendi, Ph.D., clinical psychologist and author of *You're a Better Parent than You Think* (Simon & Schuster, 1985).

It's never too early to start teaching children the value of a dollar.

Teaching children about money

Use everyday opportunities to impart your financial values, including how to save money, make it grow, and spend it wisely. Remember, your children watch and learn from your consumer and financial habits.

- As soon as your child can count (between the ages of 2 and 4), introduce her to the concept of money.

- By age 3, begin teaching the name and value of different coins.

- Play bank, store, Monopoly Junior and other money-changing games.

- Demonstrate that when you give money you get something in return: let your child put coins into a gumball machine and see what comes out.

- Ask for a tour of your local bank.

- Teach how to make change. Let your child pay for something and help her figure out how much she will get back.

- Tell your child how much you're spending when you're in the store and at the gas station. Explain what happens when you use credit cards or a cash machine.

- Let your child help clip coupons and explain how they're used. Show how you check store ads and compare prices.

- If you're short on funds, explain that you can't afford certain purchases and why. Teach your child to distinguish between things you *want* and those you *need.*

- Give your child a piggy bank. Help her set a goal to save for something special.

When to start an allowance

The best way to teach children about money is to give them an allowance. Personal finance expert Janet Bodnar suggests starting around age 6 or 7 when children begin to learn about money in school and are ready to make some purchases of their own. Let your child open a bank account to start savings habits to last a lifetime. Look for a local bank with a children's banking program.

THE EXPERT: National Center for Financial Education.

Making the most of television

Heavy viewing of television has been associated with bad eating habits, lack of exercise, poor grades and increased aggressive behavior. Yet, if used properly, TV can be an important teaching tool, increasing vocabulary and exposing children to a wide variety of information. Start healthy viewing habits early.

● Limit viewing time. (The American Academy of Pediatrics recommends no more than one to two hours a day for toddler-age children on up.)

● Involve your child in selecting the shows she can watch.

● If your child wants to watch something her friends are talking about, screen it first to make sure it's suitable. If not, explain your objections.

● Watch with your child and talk about the programs.

- Teach your child to question what she sees on TV, not to just accept everything as fact.

- Discuss what's real and what's make-believe.

- Use TV to interest your child in reading further about subjects that interest her.

- Build a library of entertaining and educational videos.

- Keep the TV in a common room to monitor its use.

- Set an example: curb your own television habits.

Children in the United States watch an average of three to five hours of television daily.

THE EXPERT: Jerome Singer, Ph.D., codirector of the Yale University Family Television Research and Consultation Center, and coauthor of *Use TV to Your Child's Advantage* (Acropolis Books, 1990).

To find appropriate and enjoyable books for your child, ask your local librarian or children's bookseller, read reviews, check lists of recommended books, and look for those that have won awards like the Caldecott or Newbery Medals.

Choosing books for your child

There are thousands of books written for children on bookstore and library shelves, but it's a challenge to choose the ones best suited to your child's age and interests, as well as those that will instill a lifelong love of reading and can be enjoyed by both parent and child over and over again.

What to  for . . .

- Simple stories that can be told in one sitting.

- Stories about everyday things and experiences plus those about special issues of concern to your child (for example, about a child getting glasses or losing a tooth).

- Characters that are the same age and sex as your child

- Real and imaginary animals and people in silly situations.

- Rhyming patterns or repeated phrases that make reading and listening fun and let children join in and read along.

 THE EXPERT: Barbara Elleman, editor of *Book Links*, an American Library Association magazine.

Classic books every preschooler should know

- *Horton Hatches the Egg*
  by Dr. Seuss (Random House)

- *The Snowy Day*
  by Ezra Jacks Keats (Viking)

- *The Story About Ping*
  by Marjorie Flack (Puffin)

- *Magic School Bus* series
  by Joanna Cole (Scholastic)

- *Make Way for Ducklings*
  by Robert McCloskey
  (Viking)

- *Where the Wild Things Are*
  by Maurice Sendak
  (HarperCollins)

- *Winnie the Pooh*
  by A. A. Milne (Dutton)

THE EXPERT: Hannah Nuba, program coordinator, The New York Public Library Early Childhood Resource and Information Center.

PLAYING

Why spend lots of money on arts-and-crafts supplies when you can get them for free? Ask your neighborhood stores, offices and factories for leftovers they may dump or sell inexpensively.

Free art supplies

▶ **Cabinetmaker or lumberyard:** wood scraps

▶ **Home decorating store:** old wallpaper books and sample paint charts

▶ **Knit shop:** yarn sample cards and end-of-lot balls of wool

▶ **Newspaper:** ends of newsprint rolls (great for big art projects — roll out on the floor or hang as a mural and lots of children can draw together)

▶ **Photo store:** plastic film canisters (perfect for storing supplies like beads, shells and glitter)

▶ **Printer:** paper in various sizes, shapes and colors

▶ **Tobacco shop:** cardboard or wooden cigar boxes to decorate

Keep a rainy day busy box stocked with catalogs, postcards, buttons, Popsicle sticks, fabric swatches, cardboard, egg cartons, stickers, wrapping paper, old calendars, yarn, toilet paper rolls, etc. Add a little glue, tape, and imagination and watch the creations appear.

THE EXPERT: Patricia Gallagher, corporate child care consultant; former elementary school teacher and preschool director; author of *Raising Happy Kids on a Reasonable Budget* (Betterway Books, 1993).

Toy box favorites 3-5 years

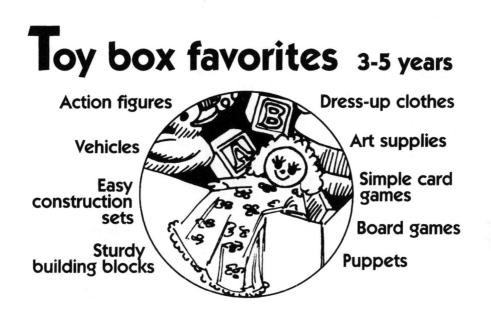

Action figures

Vehicles

Easy construction sets

Sturdy building blocks

Dress-up clothes

Art supplies

Simple card games

Board games

Puppets

Look for toys that . . .

● Provide opportunity for fantasy and imaginative play

● Boost creativity

● Allow for the development of solo play

● Foster social development, sharing and cooperating

● Teach spacial relationships and problem solving

 THE EXPERT: Helen Boehm, Ph.D., educational psychologist and toy expert, senior vice president at the MTV Network, and author of *The Right Toys* (Bantam Books, 1986).

225

Save money and let children have fun helping make these homemade recipes from common household ingredients.

Recipes for fun

Bubbles

6 cups cold water
2 cups dishwashing liquid (Joy or Dawn work well)
3/4 cup corn syrup

● Combine all ingredients. For best results, make a few days before you plan to use and refrigerate.

● For a variety of wands use plastic six-pack rings; plastic baskets that blueberries come in, or twist pipe cleaners into fun shapes — dip into bubbles and blow.

Finger paints

1 envelope unflavored gelatin
1/2 cup cornstarch
3 tablespoons sugar
2 cups cold water
food coloring
dishwashing liquid

● Soak gelatin in 1/4 cup warm water and put aside.

● In medium saucepan, combine cornstarch and sugar. Gradually add water and cook slowly over low heat, stirring until well blended.

● Remove from heat and add softened gelatin. Divide mixture into separate containers for each color. Add a few drops of food coloring and a drop or two of liquid detergent (to make cleanup easier) to each container.

● Store up to six weeks in the refrigerator.

Play dough

3 cups flour
1 1/2 cups salt
6 teaspoons cream of tartar
3 cups cool water
3 tablespoons oil
food coloring

- Mix dry ingredients together in a big pot. Blend all liquids in a bowl. Combine and cook over medium heat, stirring constantly. Remove from heat when dough pulls away from the sides of the pot and can be pinched without sticking (about five minutes).

- Turn onto a board or counter and knead until smooth. Store in an airtight container.

Goop

8 ounces white craft glue
2 cups water
food coloring
1 1/2 teaspoon borax powder

- Combine glue, one cup of water and several drops of food coloring, stirring constantly.

- In a separate bowl, combine the second cup of water and borax; stir until dissolved.

- Pour glue mixture into borax mixture, stirring until a blob forms. Knead, squeeze and play with the gooey stuff. Store in an airtight container. (Do not use on carpeting or upholstery.)

 THE EXPERT: Amy Dacyczyn, editor and publisher of *The Tightwad Gazette* newsletter.

Secrets to a successful birthday party

- Let children help plan their own parties; they'll have more fun if they're involved in the process.

- Pick a theme for invitations, decorations and games.

- Limit the guests; the younger the child, the smaller the party.

- Keep it short — two hours maximum.

- Serve simple food that children like.

- Designate another parent as official photographer.

- Begin with a quiet activity to keep arriving guests busy: hang a large sheet of paper and have everyone draw a picture or write a message to the birthday child.

- Keep order with planned activities like arts-and-crafts projects, storytelling and scavenger hunts.

- Decide beforehand if your child can open gifts at the party. If so, do it at the end.

- Prepare your child for the party by explaining what will happen. Teach her to say thank you when she receives each gift and to thank guests for coming when they leave.

- For great thank-you notes, write a message on the back of a photo of your child opening or using the gift from the person you're thanking.

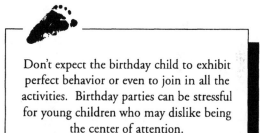

Don't expect the birthday child to exhibit perfect behavior or even to join in all the activities. Birthday parties can be stressful for young children who may dislike being the center of attention.

THE EXPERT: Meredith Brokaw, creator of Penny Whistle Toys stores, New York, and coauthor of *The Penny Whistle Birthday Party Book* (Fireside, 1992).

Goody bags are the highlight of most parties. Give them out as guests leave.

Great goody bags

- Children under 3 aren't into quantity, so give them one toy, like a coloring book or puzzle. Over age 3, they like quantity, so fill bags with lots of inexpensive fun stuff, including stickers, whistles, tattoos, colored pencils and trading cards.

- Choose favors that mirror the party theme.

- Instead of sugary candy, include sugarless lollipops, mini muffins or oatmeal cookies baked on a Popsicle stick.

- Fill a pinata with goodies wrapped in individual plastic bags so each child gets one when it breaks.

- For unique favors (to be made in advance and used at the party), buy a bunch of plain baseball caps, plastic cups or juice box holders. Use craft paint to decorate with each child's name.

- Have a crafts party — the take-home goodie is the finished product. Decorate cardboard picture frames (fill with instant party pictures), paint T-shirts or make jewelry.

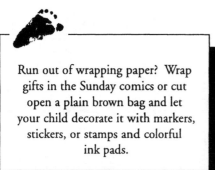

Run out of wrapping paper? Wrap gifts in the Sunday comics or cut open a plain brown bag and let your child decorate it with markers, stickers, or stamps and colorful ink pads.

 THE EXPERT: Godwyn Morris, owner of My Favorite Place, New York, an educational toy store and party room.

Selecting children's videos

Here are some age-appropriate selections for ages 4-7 that will engage you and your child:

- *Aladdin*
  (Walt Disney Home Video)

- *Dr. Seuss: The Cat in the Hat*
  (CBS/Fox Home Video)

- *E.T.*
  (Universal Home Video)

- *Free Willy*
  (Warner Home Video)

- *Strong Kids, Safe Kids*
  (Paramount Home Video)

- *The Black Stallion*
  (MGM/UA)

- *The Lion King*
  (Walt Disney Home Video)

- *The Parent Trap*
  (Walt Disney Home Video)

- *The Sound of Music*
  (20th Century Fox Home Video)

- *The Wizard of Oz*
  (MGM/UA)

 THE EXPERT: Joanna Langfield, movie critic, commentator, and host of the syndicated radio program *Joanna Langfield's Entertainment Reports.*

RESOURCES

Authors/Experts

Dr. Bob Arnot
Author of *The Best Medicine*
c/o Addison-Wesley
Publishing Co. Inc.
One Jacob Way
Reading, MA 01867-3999

Nancy Balaban
Director, Infant and Parent
Development Program
Bank Street College Graduate
School of Education
610 West 112th Street
New York, NY 10025
212-875-4400

Naomi Baron
Professor of Linguistics
Department of Language and
Foreign Studies
American University
Washington, DC 20016-8045
202-885-2381

Janet Bodnar
Senior Editor
*Kiplinger's Personal
Finance Magazine*
1729 H Street NW
Washington, DC 20006
202-887-6400

Helen Boehm
Senior Vice President
MTV Network
1515 Broadway
New York, NY 10036
212-258-8480

Meredith Brokaw
Penny Whistle Toys
448 Columbus Avenue
New York, NY 10024
212-873-9090

Dr. Joae Graham Brooks
Author of *No More Diapers!*
5950 Almaden Drive
Naples, FL 34119
941-455-5403

Robert Brooks
Director, Department of Psychology
McLean Hospital
115 Mill Street
Belmont, MA, 02178
617-855-2855

Chase Collins
Author of *Tell Me a Story*
c/o Houghton Mifflin Co.
222 Berkeley Street
Boston, MA 02116

Elizabeth Crary
Author of *Pick Up Your Socks*
c/o Parenting Press
P.O. Box 75267
Seattle, WA 98125

Amy Dacyczyn
Editor and Publisher
The Tightwad Gazette
RR1 Box 3570
Leeds, ME 04263
207-524-7962

Barbara Elleman
Editor, *Book Links*
American Library Association
50 East Huron Street
Chicago, IL 60611-2795
312-944-6780
800-545-2433

Adele Faber
Author of *Siblings Without Rivalry*
c/o Avon Books
1350 Avenue of the Americas
New York, NY 10019

Dr. Richard Ferber
Director, Center for Pediatric
Sleep Disorders
Children's Hospital — Hunnewell 2
300 Longwood Avenue
Boston, MA 02115
617-735-6663

Marilese Flusser
Author of *Party Shoes to School*
c/o Simon and Schuster
1230 Avenue of the Americas
New York, NY 10020

Nancy Friedman
The Telephone "Doctor"
30 Hollenberg Court
St. Louis, MO 63044
314-291-1012
800-882-9911

Patricia Gallagher
Author of *Raising Happy Kids on a
Reasonable Budget*
301 Holly Hill Road
Richboro, PA 18954
215-364-1945

Susan Ginsberg
Editor and Publisher
Work & Family Life
230 West 55th Street, Suite 7G
New York, NY 10019
212-265-1282

Raymond Guarendi
Author of *You're a Better Parent
Than You Think*
c/o Simon & Schuster
1230 Avenue of the Americas
New York, NY 10020

Jo-Ann Heslin
NRH Nutrition Consultants
100 Rosedale Road
Valley Stream, NY 11581
718-229-0606

Christine Heusner
Parent-Family Education
St. Luke's-Roosevelt Hospital
1000 10th Avenue
New York, NY 10019
212-523-6222

Dorothy Jordon
Editor and Publisher
Family Travel Times
40 Fifth Avenue
New York, NY 10011
212-477-5524

Dr. Patricia Keener
Safe Sitter, Inc.
1500 North Ritter Avenue
Indianapolis, IN 46219-3095
317-355-4888
800-255-4089

Dr. Philip C. Kendall
Director, Child and
Adolescent Anxiety Clinic
Temple University
Department of Psychology
Philadelphia, PA 19122
215-204-7165

Martha and David Kimmel
Mommy Made, Inc.
20 Mayer Drive
Montebello, NY 10901
914-368-0315

Ellen Klavan
Author of *The Vegetarian
Fact-Finder*
c/o The Little Bookroom
5 St. Luke's Place
New York, NY 10014

Carol Kushner
Shortcuts
104 West 83rd Street
New York, NY 10024
212-877-2277

Joanna Langfield
Mi-Ro Productions
340 West 55th Street
New York, NY 10019
212-757-7654

Judy Lawrence
Author of *Our Family Memories*
c/o Blue Sky Marketing, Inc.
P.O. Box 21583
St. Paul, MN 55121

Sunie Levin
Young Grandparents' Club
P.O. Box 11143
Shawnee Mission, KS 66207
913-642-8296

Leslie McMahon-Bushara
Early Childhood Coordinator
Children's Museum of Manhattan
212 West 83rd Street
New York, NY 10024
212-721-1234

Jeanne Miller
President, Perfectly Safe
7245 Whipple Avenue NW
North Canton, OH 44720
216-494-2323
800-837-KIDS

Godwyn Morris
My Favorite Place
265 West 87th Street
New York, NY 10024
212-362-5320

Heidi Murkoff
Coauthor of *What to Expect
When You're Expecting*
c/o Workman Publishing Co.
708 Broadway
New York, NY 10003

Dr. Karl Neumann
Traveling Healthy Newsletter
108-48 70th Road
Forest Hills, NY 11375
718-268-7290

Dr. Nelson Lee Novick
328 East 75th Street
New York, NY 10021
212-772-9300

Hannah Nuba
Program Coordinator
The New York Public Library
Early Childhood Resource and
Information Center
66 Leroy Street
New York, NY 10014
212-929-0815

John Preston
Engineering Department
U.S. Consumer Product Safety
Commission
Washington, DC 20207
202-504-0494

Beverly Roman
Author of *Moving Minus Mishaps*
BR Anchor Publishing
P.O. Box 176
Hellertown, PA 18055-0176

Robert Schachter
150 East 56th Street
New York, NY 10022
212-308-1666

Dr. Charles Schaefer
The Better Sleep Clinic
Fairleigh Dickinson University
139 Temple Avenue
Hackensack, NJ 07601
201-692-2645

Dr. Donald Schiff
Pediatrics, Denver Children's Hospital
1056 East 19th Street
Denver, CO 80218
303-837-2745

Madeleine Sigman-Grant
Assistant Professor
Department of Food Science
Pennsylvania State University
8 Borland Lab
University Park, PA 16802
814-865-5444

J. L. Simmons
Coauthor of *76 Ways to Protect
Your Child from Crime*
7336 Country Club Drive
St. Louis, MO 63121
314-382-3029

Jerome Singer
Co-Director
Yale University Family Television
Research and Consultation Center
Department of Psychology
P.O. Box 208205
New Haven, CT 06520-8205
203-432-4565

Dr. Barney Softness
450 West End Avenue
New York, NY 10024
212-769-3070

Ron Taffel
Institute for Contemporary Psychotherapy
1 West 91st Street
New York, NY 10024
212-595-3444

James Varni
Author of *Time-Out for Toddlers*
c/o Berkley Books
200 Madison Avenue
New York, NY 10016

Dr. Marc Weissbluth
680 North Lakeshore Drive, Suite 123
Chicago, IL 60611
312-642-5515

Dr. Jamie Whyte
Associate Director
Sleep Disorders Center
Columbia Presbyterian
Medical Center
161 Fort Washington Avenue
New York, NY 10032
212-305-1860

Dr. Myron Winick
Author of *Growing Up Healthy*
c/o William Morrow and Co., Inc.
1350 Avenue of the Americas
New York, NY 10019

Mildred Winter
Executive Director
Parents as Teachers National Center
10176 Corporate Square Drive
St. Louis MO 63132
314-432-4330

Companies and Organizations

Alliance to End Childhood
Lead Poisoning
227 Massachusetts Avenue NE
Suite 200
Washington, DC 20002
202-543-1147

American Academy of Dermatology
930 North Meacham Road
P.O. Box 681069
Schaumburg, IL 60168-4014

American Academy of Otolaryngology
— Head and Neck Surgery, Inc.
One Prince Street
Alexandria, VA 22314
703-836-4444

American Academy of
Pediatric Dentristy
211 E. Chicago Avenue, Suite 700
Chicago, IL 60611
312-337-2169

American Academy of Pediatrics
141 Northwest Point Boulevard
Elk Grove Village, IL 60007
847-228-5005
800-433-9016

American Association of
Poison Control Centers, Inc.
3201 New Mexico Avenue NW
Suite 310
Washington, DC 20016
202-362-7217

American College of
Emergency Physicians
11 19th Street NW
Suite 650
Washington, DC 20036
202-728-0610

American Movers Conference
1611 Duke Street
Alexandria, VA 22314
703-683-7410

American Optometric Association
243 North Lindbergh Boulevard
St. Louis, MO 63141
314-991-4100

American Podiatric
Medical Association
9312 Old Georgetown Road
Bethesda, MD 20814-1621
301-571-9200
800-366-8227

American Red Cross
National Headquarters
17th and D Street NW
Washington, DC 20006
(Call your local chapter
for information.)

American Society of
Dentistry for Children
875 North Michigan Avenue
Suite 4040
Chicago, IL 60611-1901
312-943-1244
800-637-2732

American Speech-Language-
Hearing Association
10801 Rockville Pike
Rockville, MD 20852
800-638-8255

Association for the Care
of Children's Health
7910 Woodmont Avenue, Suite 300
Bethesda, MD 20814-3015
301-654-6549
800-808-2224

Beech-Nut Nutrition Corp.
P.O. Box 618
St. Louis, MO 63188-0618
800-523-6633

Better Vision Institute
P.O. Box 77097
Washington DC 20013
703-243-1508
800-424-8422

Bicycle Federation of America
1506 21 Street NW, Suite 200
Washington, DC 20036
202-463-6622

Bicycle Helmet Safety Institute
4611 Seventh Street South
Arlington, VA 22204-1419
703-486-0100

Caring Grandparents of America
P.O. Box 96444
Washington, DC 20090-6444
800-441-7181

Child Care Aware
National Information Line
800-424-2246

Children's Hospice International
2202 Mount Vernon Avenue, Suite 3C
Alexandria, VA 22301
800-24-CHILD

Children's Nutrition Research Center
Baylor College of Medicine
1100 Bates
Houston, TX 77030
713-798-7000

Council for Exceptional Children
1920 Association Drive
Reston, VA 22091-1589
703-264-9471
800-328-0272

Depression After Delivery
P.O. Box 1282
Morrisville, PA 19067
215-295-3994
800-944-4773

Earth's Best, Inc.
4840 Pearl East Circle, Suite 201E
Boulder, CO 80301
800-442-4221

Embassy Suites
800-362-2779

EPA Safe Drinking Water Hotline
800-426-4791

Gerber Products Co.
445 State Street
Fremont, MI 49413
800-4-GERBER

Gifted Child Society
190 Rock Road
Glen Rock, NJ 07452
201-444-6530

Grandparents of America
400 Seventh Street NW, Suite 302
Washington, DC 20004
800-441-7181

International Association of
Infant Massage
5660 Clinton Street, Suite 2
Elma, NY 14059
716-684-3299
800-248-5432

International Lactation
Consultant Association
200 North Michigan Avenue
Suite 300
Chicago, IL 60601
312-541-1710

International Reading Association
800 Barksdale Road
P.O. Box 8139
Newark, DE 19714-8139
302-731-1600

Juvenile Products
Manufacturers Association
Two Greentree Centre, Box 955
Marlton, NJ 08053
609-985-2878

La Leche League International
1400 North Meacham Road
Schaumburg, IL 60173-4840
708-519-7730
800-LA-LECHE

Learning Disabilities
Association of America
4156 Library Road
Pittsburgh, PA 15234
412-341-1515

Lefthanders International Inc.
P.O. Box 8249
Topeka, KS 66608
913-234-2177

Lyme Disease Foundation, Inc.
1 Financial Plaza
Hartford, CT 06103
860-525-2000
800-886-LYME

Mayflower Transit, Inc.
P.O. Box 107
Indianapolis, IN 46206-0107
(Call your local representative.)

Maytag Consumer Education
One Dependability Square
Newton, IA 50208
515-792-7000
800-688-9900

National Association for
Gifted Children
1707 L Street NW, Suite 550
Washington, DC 20036
202-785-4268

National Association for
Family Child Care
1440-A New York Avenue NW
Suite 348
Washington, DC 20005
602-838-3446

National Association of Child Care
Resource and Referral Agencies
2116 Campus Drive SE
Rochester, MN 55904
507-287-2220

National Association
of Mothers' Centers
336 Fulton Avenue
Hempstead, NY 11550
516-486-6614
800-645-3828

National Association of Pediatric
Nurse Associates and Practitioners
1101 Kings Highway North, Suite 206
Cherry Hill, NJ 08034
609-667-1773

National Center for
Financial Education
P.O. Box 34070
San Diego, CA 92163-4070

National Center for
Learning Disabilities
381 Park Avenue South, Suite 1420
New York, NY 10016
212-545-7510

National Coalition for
School Bus Safety
c/o The Pupil Transportation
Safety Institute
443 South Warren Street
Syracuse, NY 13202
800-836-2210

National Enuresis Society
7777 Forest Lane, Suite C737
Dallas, TX 75230
800-NES-8080

National Fire Protection Association
1 Batterymarch Park
Quincy, MA 02269
800-344-3555

National Highway Traffic
Safety Administration
Auto Safety Hotline
800-424-9393

National Kidney Foundation
30 East 33rd Street
New York, NY 10016
800-622-9010

National Lead Clearinghouse
800-424-LEAD

National Lead Information Center
800-LEADFYI

National Pediculosis Association
P.O. Box 610189
Newton, MA 02161
617-449-NITS
800-446-4NPA

National Pesticide
Telecommunications Network
800-858-PEST

National Safety Council
1121 Spring Lake Drive
Itasca, IL 60143-3201
800-621-7615

National Spa and Pool Institute
2111 Eisenhower Avenue
Alexandria, VA 22314
703-838-0083
800-323-3996

National Storytelling Asssociation
P.O. Box 309
Jonesborough, TN 37659
615-753-2171
800-525-4514

Parents Information Network
for the Gifted
900-773-PING

Perfectly Safe
800-837-KIDS

Pet Loss Support Hotline
School of Veterinary Medicine
University of California, Davis
916-752-4200

Pet Loss Support Hotline
Michigan State College of
Veterinary Medicine
517-432-2696

Pittsburgh Poison Control Center
3705 Fifth Avenue
Pittsburgh, PA 15213
412-692-7104

Postpartum Support International
927 North Kellogg Avenue
Santa Barbara, CA 93111
805-967-7636

Ritz-Carlton Hotels
800-241-3333

Riverside Mothers Group
c/o Pocket Books
1230 Avenue of the Americas
New York, NY 10020

Ryder Truck Rental
3600 Northwest 82nd Avenue
P.O. Box 020816
Miami, FL 33102-0816
800-615-3999

SafetyBeltSafe U.S.A.
Box 553
Altadena, CA 91003
310-673-2666
800-745-SAFE

Safety 1st
800-962-7233

Stuttering Foundation of America
P.O. Box 11749
Memphis, TN 38111-0749
800-992-9392

Sudden Infant Death
Syndrome Alliance
1314 Bedford Avenue, Suite 210
Baltimore, MD 21208
800-221-SIDS

The American Dietetic Association
216 West Jackson Boulevard
Chicago, IL 60606-6995
800-366-1655

The American Society for the
Prevention of Cruelty to Animals
424 East 92nd Street
New York, NY 10128-6804
212-876-7700

The Council for Exceptional Children
1920 Association Drive
Reston, VA 22091
703-260-3660
800-328-0272

The Danny Foundation
3158 Danville Boulevard
P.O. Box 680
Alamo, CA 94507
800-83DANNY

The Dougy Center for
Grieving Children
P.O. Box 86852
Portland, OR 97286
503-775-5683

The Food Allergy Network
10400 Eaton Place, Suite 107
Fairfax, VA 22030-5647
703-691-3179
800-929-4040

The Safety Zone
800-999-3030

The Skin Cancer Foundation
245 Fifth Avenue, Suite 2402
New York, NY 10016
212-725-5176
800-SKIN-490

The White House
Greetings Office, Room 39
1600 Pennsylvania Avenue NW
Washington, DC 20500

Tooth Fairy Museum
1129 Cherry Street
Deerfield, IL 60015
708-945-1129
(Open by appointment only)

Toy Manufacturers of America, Inc.
200 Fifth Avenue
New York, NY 10010
212-675-1141

U.S. Consumer Product
Safety Commission
Washington, DC 20207
800-638-8270
Hotline: 800-638-CPSC

U.S. Department of Transportation
Washington, DC 20590
202-366-2220

Young Grandparents' Club
P.O. Box 11143
Shawnee Mission, KS 66207
913-642-8296

INDEX

9 780671 891992